Presented to:

_____

By:

_____

Date:

_____

Totally Awesome, Super-Cool Bible Stories

as drawn by Nerdy Ned

A Division of Thomas Nelson Publishers

NASHVILLE   DALLAS   MEXICO CITY   RIO DE JANEIRO

Published in Nashville, Tennessee, by Tommy Nelson. Tommy Nelson is a registered trademark of Thomas Nelson, Inc.

Thomas Nelson, Inc., titles may be purchased in bulk for educational, business, fund-raising, or sales promotional use. For information, please e-mail SpecialMarkets@ThomasNelson.com.

Library of Congress Cataloging-in-Publication Data

Totally awesome, super-cool Bible stories as drawn by Nerdy Ned.
   p. cm.
  ISBN 978-1-4003-2025-7 (hardcover)
  1. Bible stories, English.
  BS551.3.T67 2012
  220.9'505--dc23

2012030003

Printed in the United States of America

12 13 14 15 16 QG 6 5 4 3 2 1

www.thomasnelson.com

A Note from Ned

Hi, everyone.

My name is Ned Moses Wiley. I've always wished my parents had given me a middle name like "Super-Cool" or "Most Awesome," but as far as middle names go, I guess Moses is pretty cool. Moses listened to God and led his people out of Egypt. I think my parents were hoping my middle name would inspire similar greatness. So far the only leading I've done is to lead my cabin to a kickball victory at church camp. You gotta start somewhere, right?

This year in youth group, we worked our way through the Bible. I've gotta say—it was pretty cool. I don't think I'd ever realized just how much exciting stuff is in there. So I started drawing comics to go with each story (some people might think it's a little nerdy, but I really want to be a comic book illustrator when I grow up) and writing out all the stuff I learned. Now I present to you my first masterpiece: *Totally Awesome, Super-Cool Bible Stories As Drawn by Nerdy Ned*! (Please, please. Hold your applause.)

Seriously, the Bible is not some boring old book with stories that don't mean anything to us today. It's about a really big, awesome God who loves us a lot and did really big, awesome things—and it's a guide for how God wants us to live.

I hope reading this book makes you excited about getting to know God and about hearing what He has to say to you in the Bible. And I hope you enjoy my doodles (I even saved some space for you to draw your own).

Catch you on the flip side,
Ned Super-Cool Moses Wiley
(Hey, just wanna see how it sounds . . .)

Draw Here!

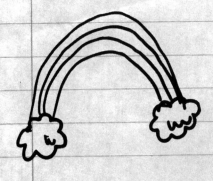

Contents
Old Testament

Contents
New Testament

Old
TESTAMENT

Draw Here!

And Then There Was Broccoli

Genesis 1

In the beginning, there was nothing, except for God. I mean, there was really NOTHING. Much worse than the kind of nothing you feel like you're staring into when you're grounded and confined to your room.

There was no land, no sea, no air, no outer space, no animals, no chocolate, no candy corn, no ice cream, no broccoli. You get the big, blank picture.

God was moving around in the nothing, and He decided to go on a massive creating spree. And it was more exciting than any 3-D movie extravaganza you've ever seen.

God said, "Let there be light!" and *boom!* Just like that, there was light. God saw that the light looked good. (Of course it looked good; God made it!) God called the light *day* and the dark *night*—end of Day One.

On Days Two and Three, God called into existence the sky and named the dry land *earth*, and the waters became *seas*. **This marks the birth of my least favorite subject—earth science.**

Then God invented farming and covered the earth in all kinds of plants. From giant redwood trees to microscopic algae and every fruit or vegetable you love or hate to eat, the whole planet was covered—just like that.

On Day Four, God decided to go nuts up in the sky. For daytime, He whipped up a flaming ball of gas called the sun. For the night, He made a cooler earth-orbiting rock called the moon. Then God dusted the entire universe with a jatrillion twinkling stars.

Too bad we can't go to the Garden of Eden for our next camping trip!

Draw Here

5

The Name Game

Genesis 1-2

God decided He wanted some creatures to live on this excellent planet, so He created animals. First, the water dwellers. He filled the seas with all sorts of slimy, scaly, swimming things. Big fish, little fish, pretty fish, ugly fish, and whales (which are mammals, not fish). Then He filled the skies with feathered, taloned, flying things. Sparrows, eagles, robins, falcons—God made them all on Day Five.

On Day Six, God made dogs and cats, beetles and arachnids, lions, bears, honey badgers, spiders, mosquitoes, ants, mice, marmots, ferrets, duckbilled platypuses, and everything else you've ever or never seen in a zoo. He made them all, and they looked good—although personally I think God probably laughed when He made the platypuses. Those things sure are funny looking.

6

After God assembled every animal ever, He still had the energy and imagination to create the coolest and most complicated being of them all: humans.

God made humans in His own image. God made two types of humans—male and female.

Then God gave those crazy kids everything. And I mean EVERYTHING.

I sure am glad God's own image didn't include a duck bill or webbed feet. Aren't you?

He actually told them to *rule* over everything on earth. The man and woman would be in charge of the plants, animals, fish—all of it! They even got to name all of the creepy, crawly, furry, and flying creatures.

God blessed the new people and said, "Look at all this good stuff I've given you."

God made it all, and it was very good. Then He took a nap—er, *rested*. God rested on the Seventh Day.

Just One Bite

Genesis 2-3

Okay, I have a confession. This next story makes me want to yell when I read it. Like when you're watching a scary movie, and the guy or girl starts walking down a creepy path alone, and you just want to scream, "Don't do that! That is the *worst* idea ever!" I want to do that every time I read this story.

So the first humans were named Adam and Eve. They had everything they could ever want in their garden of Eden home—except for the fruit of one tree.

"If you ever eat fruit from that tree, you will die," God told them.

Pretty clear, right? THIS TREE = DEATH.

Well, one day a talking snake slithered up to Eve and struck up some chitchat. "God wasn't being honest with you," the snake ← **The fact that the snake could talk should have tipped Eve off that something wasn't right.** said. "C'mon, you won't die if you eat fruit from that tree. It's good for you. You might even learn some cool stuff if you try it."

Of course, everything the sneaky snake said was a big fat lie. That snake was the ultimate con artist.

And (cue the spooky music) Eve took a bite. Then Adam showed up, and she gave some of the fruit to him, and of course, he ate it (cue louder spooky music).

THEN . . . no one choked and died a horrible death.

BUT . . .

A really bad feeling came over Adam and Eve. You know that feeling you get in the pit of your stomach when you've done something super wrong? That totally guilty, scared feeling? I think that's what it was like for Adam and Eve.

Suddenly they realized they were naked, so they threw on some fig leaf pants. They knew that what they had done was wrong, but they had never been in trouble before. Adam **← That had to have been kind of awkward.**

and Eve didn't know what God was going to do, and they were really scared. So when they heard God walking in the garden, they hid.

"Where are you?" God called.

Adam answered, "I was afraid, so I hid."

"Why are you afraid?" God asked. "Did you eat some of the fruit I told you not to eat?"

"Well, Eve ate it first. Then she gave it to me," Adam said.

God asked Eve, "What did you do?"

"The snake lied to me!" she said. "He tricked me into eating the fruit."

So God cursed the snake. And then He sent Adam and Eve out of their garden home—forever.

God told them that now they were going to have to work for the things they needed, life would be hard, and they would eventually die.

Before God sent them away, He upgraded Adam and Eve to animal-skin clothes from their sad little fig pants. Then He set an angel guard with fire swords to block the garden's gate so they could never go back. Something rotten called sin had entered the world. And we humans have been messing up ever since.

Worst. Day. Ever.

Earth 2.0

Genesis 6-9

etting kicked out of Eden was just the beginning of trouble for humans. Each new generation seemed to make things worse. People made really bad choices, did what God said was evil, and filled the world with violence.

Humans were so bad that eventually God regretted creating them. I think it's like when you're playing a video game and things get so messed up that you hit the master reset button. God wanted to hit the reset button and wipe all living creatures off the earth. But just when He thought there wasn't a single, solitary non-wicked person to be found, a righteous guy named Noah changed God's mind.

God liked the way Noah lived his life.

God told Noah about His plan to wash the world clean with a huge flood. But He also gave Noah a get-out-of-flood-free plan so he and his family could avoid being wiped out. God showed Noah how to build a gigantic boat with enough room for his whole family and two of every living creature.

Noah built the boat, gathered the animals, and hunkered down in his gopher-wood ark.

Then God hit the reset button on earth with the worst rainstorm in history.

It poured for forty days and nights, until water covered everything. But Noah's boat kept on floating. He, his family, and all the animals stayed safe. Then they floated on the water for months and months.

↑ And you think airports are crowded.

Let's be honest here. This was no luxury cruise. We're talking about living on a boat with more animals than the world's biggest zoo. You get the noisy, *stinky* picture, right?

Anyway, once the water began to go down, Noah decided to find out if it was safe to get off the boat. Of course, he couldn't just swim out and look for land, so he decided to let a bird fly away. If the bird returned with evidence of dry land, then he would know it was almost time to empty the boat.

First, Noah released a raven, but it didn't find dry land.

Next, Noah sent a dove, but it also came back to the boat empty-handed, er, empty-footed . . . empty-beaked?

Noah let the dove fly away three times. The second time, his bird friend brought back a leaf from an olive tree. The third time, it didn't come back at all. This was the sign Noah had been looking for. The flood was over.

After his family and the animals got off the boat, God spoke to Noah once more. "I will never again destroy every living thing on the earth as I did this time."

To seal the deal, God showed Noah a rainbow in the sky. And so, ROY G BIV was born. (Red, Orange, Yellow, Green, Blue, Indigo, Violet—get it?)

Draw Here!

You're Not Speaking My Language

Genesis 11

I n fifth grade, I was super-determined to win the science fair. I had the best idea for our project. All my three lab partners had to do was execute their portion of the experiment—for which I gave perfect directions—and we were sure to win.

There was no doubt in my mind that the Great Inverted Exploding Volcano would be science-fair gold. We just had to work together.

But I couldn't seem to communicate to my team what a winning idea it was to turn the classic baking soda volcano upside down. My partners could only think about getting in trouble for messing up the science lab floor. It was like they weren't speaking my language.

We all speak English, so I don't know what the problem was. It's not like we were trying to build the Tower of Babel and *literally* got struck with different languages.

Cue mass confusion. ⬅

You see, after God hit the big reset button (aka the Great Flood), people on earth began working together. It was easy because they all spoke the same language, and they discovered that they could do a lot of great things. Construction was their specialty. They put up buildings, towns, even entire cities. They became so good at construction with their fancy baked bricks and tar for mortar that their egos got really out of control. They decided to build a tower to celebrate their own awesomeness and left God totally out of their plans.

"Let's build ourselves a city and a tower," they said. "And let's make the top of the tower reach high into the sky. We will become famous!"

As you might have guessed, God wasn't happy about this project. He wanted the people to spread out over the world and to remember that they needed Him in order to survive. So God made the people speak different languages so they couldn't understand each other.

God was right. When everyone spoke different languages, the people stopped building the tower and spread out all over the world.

Draw Here ↓

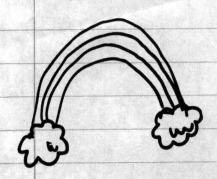

The First Two Ridiculously Old People to Have a Baby

Genesis 17; 21

I really hate it when my mom and dad get all misty-eyed about when I was born. They love to talk about what a miracle I was— er, am. I guess people thought Mom and Dad were too old to have more kids because they both have what is called "premature gray" hair. And they already had my big sister, Penelope, who was six years old when I came along.

← I sure do hope he likes kids.

When my parents start the Ned-was-a-big-surprise sap-fest, I just remind them they were not the first sort-of-old people to have a baby.

Abram and his wife, Sarai, wanted to have a baby, but they had major doubts that it would happen for them. This was understandable because by the time most people have grandkids, Abram and Sarai hadn't even had their first child.

When Abram was ninety-nine years old, God made him a promise: "If you listen to Me and do what is right, I promise that you will become the father of many nations."

← Yes, Ninety-nine.

Abram was blown away by this good news. He bowed down and worshipped God.

God said He would give Abram a huge family: kids, grandkids, great-grandkids, great-great-grandkids—a truly massive family tree. Abram's family would include entire nations, even kings.

Then, to help Abram remember the promise, God gave him a new name.

"You won't be Abram anymore," God said. "You'll be Abraham. I'm changing your wife's name too. From now on, Sarai will be Sarah. And Sarah is going to have a son!"

I sure hope they liked their new names, because when God changes your name, you don't have much of a choice in the matter!

Best kick in the stomach ever.

Just like God said she would, Sarah had a baby. It was a little boy.
The baby was named Isaac, which means "laughter." That name was totally appropriate because, let's face it, even in the Bible, having a baby when you're one hundred years old is pretty funny.

ᒺ**Does this mean Abraham was 105 when Isaac started kindergarten?**

Double Trouble

Genesis 25-33

I've always imagined what it would be like to have an identical twin. There is so much I could accomplish if I only had to go to half of the boring stuff like Mom's garden society shows or Dad's stamp collector conventions. My twin and I would also make the smartest tag team in professional wrestling history: Ned and Ted, the Wiley Brothers.

We would be nothing like Jacob and Esau, the twin boys of Abraham's son Isaac and his wife, Rebekah. The brothers did not get along—mainly because Jacob was a total jerk. Jacob lied, stole, and cheated Esau out of everything that should have been his. And Esau . . . well, he wasn't very charming either.

The brothers really became enemies when Jacob pulled off a major swindle and took their father Isaac's blessing away from Esau. Esau was ready to kill Jacob. Like, seriously, not just what brothers say when they are mad. But sneaky Jacob ran away. They both grew up, became successful, had families of their own, and didn't see each other again for many years.

God told Jacob to take his family and his animals and head back home. He sent some messengers ahead of him to meet Esau . . .

"Hey, Boss," Jacob's workers told him. "Your brother is in town, and he's got an army of four hundred really big dudes with him."

Jacob figured Esau was finally coming to kill him, so he sent a huge present to Esau with a Hey-Don't-Hurt-Me card attached.

And then Jacob went to sleep, but not for long.

> IF GOD DECIDES TO CHANGE MY NAME, I HOPE IT'S TO CAPTAIN AWESOME

In the middle of the night, a stranger woke Jacob up, and he wanted to fight. The two wrestled for hours. During the fight, the stranger injured Jacob's hip, but Jacob never gave up.

Finally, the stranger said, "Let me go. The sun is coming up."

"Only if you bless me," Jacob said.

Then the stranger asked Jacob his name, and what happened next blew Jacob's mind.

"You're getting a new name," the stranger said. "From now on, people will call you Israel because you have fought with God and with men and you have won."

"What's your name?" Jacob asked.

But the stranger never told him. He just gave Jacob a blessing. Jacob realized that he had just seen God face-to-face.

←You'll want to remember this name for later.

Then he looked up and saw Esau coming with his Really Big Dude army.

With a messed-up hip and worn out from stranger-fighting, Jacob prepared for the worst from the brother he had wronged so badly.

But guess what? Surprise ending: Esau didn't want to kill his brother; he wanted to give him a really big hug. Esau had already forgiven Jacob.

Draw Here↓

Sibling Rivalry: Extreme Edition

Genesis 37

Everybody knows that parents are not supposed to have favorite children. My parents are pretty good at treating my sister, Penelope, and me the same, even though she is quite a bit older. When she got a car for her sixteenth birthday, they got me a new bike with a card that said, "We love you both the same, dear." (Penelope and I agree that her pre-owned clunker is as much of a rust bucket as my wreck-on-wheels ten-speed. So they definitely treated us equally on the transportation front.)

Jacob apparently wasn't aware of the no-favorites rule. He was a terrible brother when he was younger, so it's really no surprise that he turned out to have a few challenges when it came to being a good dad. Jacob had a lot of sons, but he had one favorite: his second-youngest son, Joseph.

Joseph was a good guy, but his brothers hated him because their dad treated him way better than he treated them. When Jacob gave Joseph a very expensive and awesome present—a fancy, colorful robe—his brothers got super mad.

Just what I've always wanted—a fancy striped bathrobe.

One day, Jacob sent Joseph to the place where his brothers were working to check up on them. When they saw Joseph coming, the brothers planned to kill him. Jealousy can make people do some seriously crazy things. They would have done it, too, but Joseph's brother Reuben spoke up for him.

"Let's not kill him," Reuben said. "Throw him into this empty well here in the desert. But don't hurt him!"

Reuben, the brother who wasn't infected with the green-eyed envy disease, realized that his brothers weren't thinking so clearly. He thought that once everybody calmed down, he'd go get Joseph out of the hole and bring him home.

When Joseph reached them, the brothers ripped off Joseph's fancy coat and threw him into the empty well. Then, as they sat down to have some dinner, some slave traders passed by. Reuben had stepped away somewhere and wasn't around to protect his young brother, so Joseph's brothers sold him to some slave traders. Joseph was taken to Egypt—far from their home.

← **I imagine he had stepped out to make one of his famous namesake sandwiches.**

If Pen sold me into slavery, my parents would ground her for life.

27

VIP Joseph

Genesis 39-41

You know the "I Survived Bullying" stories we hear all the time at special school assemblies about how important it is to be nice to each other? Well, Joseph's survival tale is one of the best.

Despite starting out as a slave, Joseph actually made a pretty good life for himself in Egypt. Things went well for Joseph until the wife of his boss, an important Egyptian leader, accused him of some stuff he didn't do and put him in prison. Not cool. God showed His favor to Joseph even when he was in prison. He gave him the ability to interpret dreams.

One night, the king of Egypt had a dream that he didn't understand. He called in his closest advisors and told them about it, but they weren't any help either. No one could explain the dream, but one of the men Joseph had helped in jail remembered him and told the king that Joseph might be able to figure it out.

"Can you help me?" the king asked Joseph.

"*I* can't," Joseph said. "But if you tell me your dream, God will."

The king said he saw seven fat cows and seven skinny cows in his dream. Then he saw seven beautiful, healthy stalks of grain and seven raggedy stalks of grain.

What did it all mean?

With God's help, Joseph knew the answer.

Joseph told the king that the fat cows and healthy plants meant that Egypt would have seven very good and productive years. But the seven years after that would be really bad. People wouldn't have enough food

to eat. Skinny cows and puny grain = hard times. Get it? Joseph told the king and his people to save during the good years so that they could make it through the bad.

The king was super grateful for Joseph's help. He was so grateful that he promoted Joseph from a prisoner to right-hand man. The king told all the Egyptians that Joseph ⬅ was in charge of the kingdom. "Go to Joseph. Do whatever he tells you to do."

He even gave Joseph a flashy ring to mark his VIP status.

And that's what they did. For seven years, people had more than enough of what they needed, but they didn't waste anything. They saved so that when the bad years came, the people in Egypt had enough to eat.

Draw Here

Family Reunion Forgiveness

Genesis 41-45

Remember back when I told you Joseph was a good guy? Well, he *really* should have won a good guy medal, and this is where he proved it.

Thanks to Joe's leadership, the people in Egypt had enough food to eat during the seven bad years. But back in his home in Canaan, things were really rough.

There was no food in the whole country, and Joseph's family was hungry. His father, Jacob, sent Joseph's brothers to Egypt to find some supplies. As soon as they showed up, Joseph recognized them. But they didn't recognize him.

Seeing his brothers made him remember everything that they had done to him—how they hurt him and took him away from his father. It was the perfect chance for revenge.

But that's not what Joseph did. After seeing them several times, he said, "I am your brother Joseph. You sold me as a slave. Now, don't worry. Don't be angry with yourselves because you sold me. God sent me here ahead of you to save people's lives." **← Insert surprised gasps here.**

God helped Joseph to forgive the brothers who had bullied him and treated him so badly. Guess I better forgive with that kid who called me "Ned, Ned, stupidhead" in fourth grade.

Bring Your Own Basket

Exodus 2

My sister, Penelope, used to read these books about babysitting. From what I can tell, some girls with different colors of hair made a club so they could yap about the little kids they took care of. Not that I would *know* because I *never* read *those* books. Anyway, I'm pretty sure you would get kicked out of their club if you tried floating a kid down the river in a basket. But Exodus says that's what the mom of a baby named Moses had to do.

When Moses was just three months old, some very powerful people wanted to kill all the Hebrew baby boys in Egypt. Moses' mom was desperate to save him. That's why she put him in a floating basket and sent it down the river. She was hoping that God would lead someone to her baby to protect him.

The daughter of Egypt's king found the basket with baby Moses in it crying. The Egyptian princess saw that he was one of the Hebrew babies who was in danger and decided to help him. Moses' sister had stayed close by to watch what happened. She went up to the princess and asked if she wanted a nurse to help her with the baby.

Wouldn't you be crying if your mom floated you down the river in a basket—in crocodile country—without a bottle or a rattle to keep you entertained?

"Yes, please," the princess said. Of course Moses' sister got his mom to be his nurse. His mother cared for him and loved him. When Moses got older, his mother took him back to the king's daughter. She adopted him and named him Moses, which means "drew him from the water."

Warning: Do not try this with your little brother or sister.

Warning: Fire NOT to Be Used for Making S'mores

Exodus 2-3

When Moses grew up, he realized that the king of Egypt didn't treat everyone in his kingdom fairly. He made the Israelite people slaves. They had to work very hard, were not paid, and had no rights. That wasn't cool with Moses. He had been born an Israelite, so he thought that the Israelites should be free.

One day Moses tried to help an Israelite man who was in trouble, but he messed things up—real bad. Moses killed the Egyptian who was beating a Hebrew slave, and Moses had to leave the kingdom. No more royal palace for him. He started over in a place called Midian, where he became a shepherd.

Years after leaving Egypt, Moses was in the field with his flock of sheep when he saw something he'd never seen before. A nearby bush was on fire, but it wasn't burning up, so Moses investigated. **Wouldn't YOU investigate a burning bush that wasn't, well, burning?** ←

Before he reached the bush, though, he heard a voice—a huge, bone-shaking voice. It was the voice of God—calling his name.

"Moses, Moses!"

Quaking, Moses said, "Here I am."

First, God told Moses to take off his shoes because he was in a holy place. Then God formally introduced Himself.

"I am the God of your ancestors. I am the God of Abraham, the God of Isaac, and the God of Jacob."

God wanted Moses to go back to Egypt and help not just one person, but all the people who were hurting.

"I have seen the troubles my people have suffered in Egypt," God said. "And I have heard their cries when the Egyptian slave masters hurt them. I have come down to save them from the Egyptians.

"So now I am sending you to the king of Egypt. Go! Bring My people, the Israelites, out of Egypt!"

If my mom and dad used a burning bush to get my attention, I might put down my video games a little quicker. Just sayin' . . .

I THINK SOMEONE IS TRYING TO GET YOUR ATTENTION, MAN.

Plague-a-palooza

Exodus 7-12

Moses did what God had asked him to do. He went back to Egypt with his brother Aaron. Moses told the king that God wanted him to set the Israelite slaves free.

God said Aaron could tag along for moral support.

Now, remember when you were little and your parents would say, "I'm going to count to three, and then you better [insert whatever you were refusing to do here]"? With every number, did you get a little more afraid of what would happen to you if you didn't do what they said? I think the king of Egypt failed to learn that lesson when he was a kid.

The king refused to set the Israelites free. He was incredibly stubborn.

God started one of those "countdowns" you might remember—only much scarier.

First, God told Moses and Aaron to stretch their walking sticks out over the water of the Nile River.

They did what God asked, and the water turned into blood. *Blood!* The people couldn't drink it, the fish couldn't swim in it, and it smelled rotten. The Nile was nasty.

But the king would not let the Israelites go.

So God filled Egypt with frogs. Frogs were everywhere—in the streets, in the yard, in the house, even in the king's palace. Imagine finding a bunch of frogs in your bathtub or your bed or your fridge! Gross!

Fed up, the king promised that he would let the Israelites go if Moses and Aaron made the frogs go away. With God's help, they did.

But as soon as the frogs were gone, the king changed his mind. He still would not let the people go.

↑ **This is seriously gross!**

So God filled Egypt with gnats—those teeny, tiny bugs that buzz in your face and fly up your nose and get in your eyes—but the king didn't care.

Then God filled Egypt with flies. Once again, the king told Moses that if he stopped *this plague*, then he would let the people go. But, of course, it was a trick.

Worse things followed.

God caused the Egyptians' farm animals to get sick and die.

God caused boils to cover people's bodies.

God caused a huge hailstorm.

God filled Egypt with locusts.

God turned the sky dark in the middle of the day.

And after all that . . . the king *still* would not let the people go.

Seriously, the king seems a little dense.

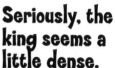

Then God filled Egypt with terrible sadness. All of the firstborn sons of the Egyptians died, even the king's son. Nothing happened to the Israelites, though, because God warned them and told them to put a special sign over their door to show that they were followers of God so their sons would be spared.

That did the trick. Finally, the king let God's people go.

A Divine Shortcut

Exodus 14

Have you ever heard the expression "No backsies"? As in, you can't take back what you said or did? I guess that wasn't much of a thing in Egypt, because the king had a habit of breaking promises.

Right after the Israelites left Egypt, the king changed his mind—again—about letting them go.

"What have we done? We let the people of Israel leave. We have lost our slaves!"

Mule King loaded up six hundred of his chariots with army guys and chased after the Israelites to the shores of the Red Sea. He intended to bring them back by force.

I am now renaming the king of Egypt "Mule King." Because ◄ he was as stubborn as a mule. Get it?

The Israelite people were scared. They knew the Egyptian army was chasing them and there was a giant, deep sea in front of them. They complained to Moses, "What have you done to us? We would rather live as slaves in Egypt than die here next to the sea."

But Moses knew God had a plan.

"Keep calm. The Lord will fight for you."

Talk about staying cool under pressure! With the king's army getting closer and closer, Moses followed God's instructions and walked to the edge of the sea and held his walking stick over the water.

God sent a strong east wind. The wind was so powerful that it caused the sea to split. God made a path forward for Moses and the Israelites. They crossed the Red Sea without even getting their feet wet.

When the king's army reached the shore, they saw the path too. They tried to follow in the Israelites' steps.

Huge, HUGE mistake.

Once the whole army was in the sea, God told Moses to stretch out his hands over the sea again, and He made the water come crashing back down over the path. The sea wiped out the king's entire army. Not one person was left alive.

The Israelites were headed to the Promised Land. But it was gonna be kind of a long trip.

Draw Here!

All-You-Can-Eat Manna

Exodus 16

With Egypt and the Red Sea behind them, Moses and the Israelites faced a new challenge—they had to walk across a desert. The Bible says this place was called the Desert of Sin, which I find odd.

Or appropriate.

Or both.

I mean, in a place called "Sin," you might guess that it was hot and dirty and there wasn't enough food for everybody to eat. And that's exactly what the desert was like.

The hot, dirty, hungry people complained to Moses. A lot.

"Hey, Moses. At least we had food in Egypt."

But Moses knew that God had a plan.

God made food fall from the sky. How awesome would that be?! He covered the ground with small white seeds or flakes of bread called manna. The people would gather the manna they needed for their families for that day. If the people followed God's plan, they would have food to eat every day, even in the desert.

Nachos from heaven. Mmmm.

The Israelites still managed to complain though . . .

44

Draw Here↓

H₂Oh, My Goodness

Exodus 17

I guess all that manna made the people thirsty because it wasn't too long after God starting feeding them that they began to complain to Moses about not having enough water to drink. Needy bunch.

"Hey, Moses. At least we had water to drink in Egypt."

The people still didn't realize that God had a plan for them. My dad would say the Israelites' complaining had now entered "whining territory." Dad says, "One complaint is a need. Two complaints is you're annoying. Three or more complaints is you're never gonna get you what you want."

But even though the Israelites were whining, God still gave them what they needed. He told Moses to tap a rock with his walking stick. Moses did this while the people watched, and when he hit the rock, water began to pour out of it. So God made water come out of rocks and food fall from the sky. I usually hate camping, but I think this would be an excellent way to do it.

Draw Here

Draw Here!

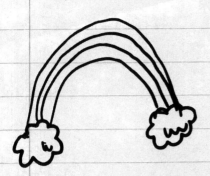

Layin' Down the Law

Exodus 19-20

Y ou know how at the beginning of school year, teachers hand out rules for behavior and other laws for living in their classroom? This year, one teacher, Mrs. MacRigor, took a whole new approach.

On our first day, she told us we'd be spending the week in "Classroom Contract Negotiations." Everybody had to write down rules that we thought would help us get the most out of sixth-grade social studies. There were lots of unoriginal submissions like "No gum in class" and "No passing notes."

But I wanted more out of the Classroom Contract—I mean, if we had to have rules, they might as well be interesting. So I recommended that we have "Pogo Stick Wednesdays." Everyone would spend the period bouncing on pogo sticks while reciting state capitals or countries or whatever we were memorizing that week.

I had excellent support from many of my fellow students. But Mrs. MacRigor totally rejected my ideas. She said Pogo Stick Wednesdays wasn't a rule; it was a plan for chaos.

Anyway, Mrs. MacRigor cracked under the pressure of trying to include all of our ridiculous ideas. We ended up with the same list of rules she had used the year before. Outside of the "no jokes about historical figures" rule, I think the basic guide is pretty fair. They're based on the Ten Commandments, after all.

God didn't ask for ideas from the Israelites for His rules for living. He called up Moses and told him His plan.

Moses climbed Mount Sinai, above where the Israelites were camped. At the top he heard God's voice.

"Moses, now that I have brought the people out of Egypt, ask them if they will obey Me and keep My agreement. If they say yes, then they will be My chosen people."

Moses came off the mountain and delivered God's message. The leaders of the people agreed to do everything God said.

Moses gave God the people's answer. Then God spoke.

I am the Lord your God. I brought you out of the land of Egypt where you were slaves.
- *You must not have any other gods.*
- *You must not make any idols.*
- *You must not use the name of the Lord your God thoughtlessly.*
- *Remember the Sabbath and keep it holy.*
- *Honor your father and your mother.*
- *You must not murder anyone.*
- *You must not commit adultery.*
- *Your must not steal.*
- *You must not tell lies.*
- *You must not want to take your neighbor's things.*

The people heard thunder, saw lightning, and watched smoke rising from the mountain. They were terrified and told Moses, "Speak to us yourself. Then we will listen. But don't let God speak to us, or we will die."

And Moses told the people, "Don't be afraid. God has come to test you. He wants you to respect Him so you will not sin."

Mooooo!

Exodus 32

It's a good thing God didn't ask the Israelites for suggestions when He was writing His rules for living. They broke the first commandment before they even saw the list. While Moses was on the mountain talking with God, the people got tired of waiting for him to come down.

They went to Aaron, Moses' second-in-command, and said, "Moses led us out of Egypt, but we don't know what has happened to him. So make us a god who will lead us."

I guess Aaron had lost faith in Moses too—and his mind, for that matter—because he agreed. The people melted down all of their gold—earrings, necklaces, belt buckles, and everything else. Once the gold was melted, Aaron took it and made a statue of a calf. The people cheered, "This is your god who brought you out of Egypt!"

Meanwhile, on the mountain, God told Moses that the people had started worshipping a golden calf and that there was serious sinning going on. Needless to say, God was very angry.

So Moses came down from the mountain. He brought the Ten Commandments with him, chiseled on two stone tablets. When Moses saw the calf and how the people were acting, he was *not* happy. Moses went all angry action hero and smashed the tablets. Then he destroyed the calf made of gold.

But God was still angry with the people because of what they had done. Terrible things happened to the Israelites because of their sin.

Draw Here ↓

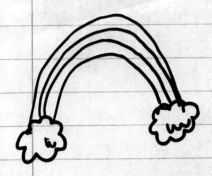

When a Donkey Talks, You'd Better Listen

Numbers 22

My parents are always telling me, "The choices you make today will affect your life tomorrow." They even make me sit down and do these goal-setting activities to help keep me on the right track. I *hate* goal-setting activities, so I told them they should hire Balaam's talking donkey to make sure I didn't step out of line. They thought I was just being a smart aleck at first. But I explained to them that if they just *read their Bibles* they would know what I was talking about.

That WAS a little smart alecky, I must admit. Whoops!

You see, Balaam's life was going in the wrong direction. He was riding his donkey to a place God didn't want him to go.

God was so upset with Balaam that He sent an angel—who happened to be carrying a very sharp sword—to block the road. Balaam couldn't see the angel, but his donkey could. Apparently the donkey liked Balaam and didn't want him to get his head chopped off, so she turned off the road to get out of the angel's way.

Balaam got angry that the donkey had veered off path. He hit that poor donkey until she went back on the road.

A little while later, the donkey saw the angel again. This time the animal moved to the edge of the road and caused Balaam to crush his foot against a wall.

Balaam got even angrier and hit his donkey again.

A little farther on down the road, the donkey saw the angel again. This time the animal just laid down.

Balaam was furious and hit his donkey a third time.

But then something pretty amazing happened.

"What is your problem, Balaam?" said THE DONKEY. "Why do you keep hitting me?"

"Because you're making me look bad!" Balaam said. "If I had a sword I would kill you!"

You know what else is crazy about this story? Balaam just answered the donkey instead of completely

freaking out, which most definitely is what I would have done. I mean, the donkey was TALKING, for crying out loud. But Balaam and that donkey, they just kept chatting.

"I am your very own donkey. You have ridden me for years. Have I ever done this to you before?"

"No," Balaam admitted.

Suddenly, Balaam saw the angel too, and he realized that he had messed up.

"Why do you keep hitting your donkey when you should be thanking her?" said the angel. "If it had not been for her, you would have run into me, and that would have been bad for you. I know you are going the wrong way."

Balaam realized that he was wrong. And he was finally ready to listen and do what God wanted. And hopefully he was much nicer to his donkey! I know I would have been.

God's Super-Secret Victory Plan

Joshua 6

I am a master of video games. Seriously, I rank way high in almost all of the games we play on the sixth-grade network. My best strategy always involves some kind of sneak attack or invisibility shield. When I first read about Joshua, the guy who took over as the leader of the Israelites after Moses, and God's strategy to conquer Jericho, I was shocked. As a skilled video game warrior, I would have had some serious doubts about God's plan.

God told Joshua that the city would belong to the Israelites if they followed His instructions. Then He gave Joshua a super-secret victory plan to share with his people. God told Joshua to have his army march around the city's walls one time every day for six days. They were not allowed to talk or shout, and they definitely could not start a fight. The only sound they could make was to blow their trumpets. Then on the seventh day, they would be doing things a little differently.

Joshua gave his army these instructions. I wonder if they thought Joshua was a little loony or, as my grandmother would say, one sandwich short of a picnic.

But whatever they thought of the plan, they followed it. On the first day, the army did as Joshua commanded. They marched around the city one time without talking, shouting, or starting a fight. They only blew their trumpets.

On the second day, they did the same thing.

For six days they followed the same order—marching around the city once and blowing their trumpets.

I bet those folks inside the walls were thinking they were pretty

safe. I mean, how threatening could a little marching and horn blowing be? Our middle school marching band does that, and they've never
taken over a city.

The seventh day started like the rest. Joshua's army marched
around the city once just like they had the previous six days, but this
time, they didn't stop. They kept going.

Two times.

Three times.

Four, five, six times around the city, and then on the seventh lap,
the army finally got to yell and scream.

And when they screamed, the walls of Jericho came tumbling
down. Joshua's army won the battle because they listened to God.

God's plan seemed kind of nuts. But you can't question the
results—those walls came a-tumblin' down, like the church song goes,
and they took the city.

One ferocious
marching band

The Lady Judge

Judges 4

Not too long ago, Penelope dated a total loser. His name was Thad, and everyone called him "Big Bad Thad." (That should have been her first clue that he was a lo-ser.) To make a long, sappy story short, she thought she was his one and only girlfriend. But when she met him at the entrance to their junior prom, it turned out she was one of five girls he had asked.

After the Great Prom Incident, Penelope locked herself in her room and cried for three days. Then, out of nowhere, she emerged from her room dressed completely in black. Penelope announced she would now go by the name "Deborah" (pronounced de-BOR-uh). She said she was going to become a very "serious woman of power." My mom got all teary-eyed and started playing songs from the 1970s. I just wanted to know where she came up with the new name.

Turns out Penelope had been reading about this woman in the Bible named Deborah. There were twelve judges in Israel, and she was the only lady judge. She would meet people under her palm tree, hear their problems, and give them a solution.

Not all of the Israelites' issues could be solved from Deborah's palm tree court. Their biggest problem was a bad king named Jabin and his general, Sisera, aka General Jerk, who ruled over them. With God's help, Deborah came up with a plan to defeat Jabin and General Jerk.

Deborah called for Barak, one of the leaders of her people's army. She told him where to take his troops and what to do when he got there. Barak was so impressed with Deborah that he insisted she go with him into the battle. She agreed but told Barak that people might make fun of him for having a woman military advisor.

"You will not get credit for the victory," Deborah told Barak. "The Lord will let a woman defeat Sisera."

Barak did everything Deborah told him to do. Israel defeated Jabin and General Jerk.

Penelope survived the Great Prom Incident too. She wasn't distracted with Big Bad Thad anymore, and she put all of her energy into becoming senior class president. Her campaign promises included background checks for potential prom dates and all-white-meat chicken nuggets in the cafeteria. As a woman of power, she got the school to agree to the chicken nuggets. The prom date background checks are still pending.

Gideon the Unimpressive

Judges 6-7

Remember when I told you that I was a video game master? Well, my physical abilities do not match my battle strategy talent. I rely on brains instead of muscle.

This guy named Gideon in the Bible was kind of an unimpressive figure too. When the angel of the Lord appeared to him and said, "The Lord is with you, mighty warrior," Gideon had doubts.

First of all, he wasn't a warrior; he worked on his family's farm. Second, he was a nobody in a family of nobodies. He wasn't exactly the kind of person soldiers followed into battle. Third, things were so difficult for Gideon and God's people at the time that he doubted God was with him or anybody else.

"Pardon me, sir," Gideon said. (Gideon was very polite.) "If the Lord is with us, why are we having so many troubles? Our ancestors told us

ARE YOU SURE I'M THE RIGHT ONE FOR THE JOB?

He did miracles. They told us the Lord brought them out of Egypt. But now He has left us. He has allowed the Midianites to defeat us."

"You have the strength to save the people of Israel. I am the one who is sending you," the Lord told him.

After some convincing, Gideon agreed to go

up against Israel's enemies. Of course, God had another impressive and original battle plan.

He told Gideon to take a very small army— **Again with the trumpets?** just three hundred men—to the Midianites' camp. Gideon gave each guy a trumpet and an empty jar with a burning torch in it.

"Surround the enemy camp," Gideon told his men. "My group will blow our trumpets, and you blow your trumpets. Then yell, 'For the Lord and for Gideon!'"

Gideon and the tiny army got to the enemy camp in the middle of the night. (Perfect time for a sneak attack.) They blew their trumpets and smashed their jars. With their torches in their left hands and the trumpets in their right hands, they yelled, "A sword for the Lord and for Gideon!" They stayed in their places—they didn't run in and attack the camp.

When Gideon's three hundred men blew their trumpets, God caused all the men of Midian to turn and fight each other with their swords. The enemy army finally just ran away.

Never underestimate a scrawny guy with a battle plan from God.

Tiny army. BIG noise!

Samson and His Hairy Problem

Judges 15-16

Now, let me be clear. Just because I am not a muscle king myself doesn't mean I don't like them. My best friend, Austin, is the second-biggest kid in the sixth grade. He's a massive force on the soccer team. But unlike me, who has to work for the attention of girls, Austin is always surrounded by them. It's kind of a distraction, especially since he's too nice to tell any of them to get lost. Our soccer coach keeps telling him all the attention from the ladies is going to ruin his focus. Coach said since I wasn't distracted with girls that I should help Austin ignore them too.

So I sat Big A down and told him about Samson. Samson was strong—so strong that he once took down one thousand pesky Philistines (the enemies of Israel in Samson's time) by himself. And—I'm not making this up—he killed them all with a donkey bone.

But Samson fell in love with a beautiful woman named Delilah. Too bad she was a spy for the Philistines, on a mission to find out what made him so strong.

Guess how she found out the secret to Samson's strength? *She asked him.* Yep, all she did was ask, and Samson told her everything. (I said he was strong—not smart.) At first, Samson managed to avoid letting the cat out of the bag. He made up some crazy stories about different ways he could be tied up that would make him weak. But eventually Delilah wore him down, and he told her the truth.

"It's my hair," he said. "I've never had a haircut, and if I ever did, I'd lose my strength."

So guess what happened the next time Samson fell asleep? Yep, he woke up with a shaved head and was captured by the Philistines. They threw him in prison and did lots of terrible things to him, including plucking out his eyes.

But Samson's enemies made a big mistake. They forgot to keep his head shaved. The longer they kept him in prison, the longer his hair grew, and the stronger he became.

One day the Philistines were having a big party in their fancy temple. They dragged Samson out of his cell to make fun of him.

Samson prayed while they laughed. "Lord God, remember me, and please give me strength one more time."

Then Samson pushed against two pillars that were holding up the roof. He shoved as hard as he could until the ceiling fell, killing himself and everyone else in the building. Samson killed more Philistines that day than he ever had before.

As for Big A, he is now officially afraid of girls. He is also growing out his hair. We'll see if it leads to a middle school soccer championship.

No, seriously. Very impressive, Samson.

Draw Here!

67

"I'm Sticking With You"

Ruth 1

ig A has been my best friend since the fourth grade. I met him at the lowest point of my twelve short years on earth. I was in trouble for cheating on a math test. I know, I know—cheating is BAD! I had a weak moment, and I've never done it again.

You see, I'm not a numbers guy, and Lydia, the girl who sat beside me, had really huge handwriting. So it was easy for me to do the stretch-and-look without being too obvious about it. I made an *exact copy* of everything Lydia wrote down on her tests. Including the hearts and stars at the end of each equation. Not sure why I did that. But then, I wasn't being smart by cheating in the first place. I never had a chance of getting that past old eagle eyes, Mr. Polly.

He sent me to the principal's office for detention as soon as he took up the tests.

I was nearly dying of guilt when Austin came and sat beside me on the couch outside Principal Irvin's office. Austin had to go home early because he was sick. I know he wasn't faking it because he looked really green. Anyway, when Principal Irvin came out to get me, she saw how bad Austin looked and asked him if he was okay. Austin stood up to talk to her and threw up on her shoes. Principal Irvin was so grossed out that she ran to the bathroom and totally forgot that I was there for detention. I guess her mind got wiped clean from the trauma of being thrown up on.

After that, I figured I pretty much owed Austin my life. To pay him back, I collected all of the icee-pops we had in our freezer and took them to him, since he was stuck at home with strep throat. We've been loyal friends ever since.

There are a bunch of stories in the Bible about loyalty. My favorite is about this woman named Naomi. She had a husband, two sons, and two daughters-in-law.

However, tragedy struck Naomi when, in a short period of time, her husband and both sons died, leaving the three ladies to fend for themselves. This wasn't easy to do in Bible times.

Since Naomi loved her daughters-in-law like they were her own children, she wanted what was best for them. She told them to leave her and find new husbands.

"There's no good reason for you to stay with me," Naomi said. "Go and find someone that you can start a family with."

One left, but the other, named Ruth, decided to stay with Naomi. Ruth loved Naomi like her own mom and said that she would never leave her.

"I promise that wherever you go, I'm going with you," Ruth said. "Your people will be my people, and your God will be my God. Please don't ever ask me to leave you behind. We're in this together." You know what? God took care of them and really blessed them.

I think Big A and I will be sticking together for a long time too.

Things Aren't What They Seem

1 Samuel 1

Recently I had to go with my mom to a night meeting at church. This committee she works on was supposed to meet our new pastor for the first time, and she doesn't trust me to stay at home by myself yet. Penelope and my dad were off doing some father-daughter bonding time.

So I just hung out on the front steps of the church while she was in the meeting.

As I stared out into the parking lot, bored out of my mind, I noticed this guy pacing back and forth in front of an old beat-up car. He was talking on a cell phone and looking up and down the road in front of the church.

I got a little nervous because I had heard on the news there was a prison break earlier in the week. Over the next few minutes, I convinced myself this guy was an escaped axe murderer planning his next move.

Then he saw me from across the lot and yelled, "Hey, kid! I've got a question for you," and started jogging toward me.

I jumped up and ran inside to find my mom. I busted into the meeting room and could barely breathe. All I could say was, "Crazy dude! Cra-zee dude!"

Everyone in the room stood up, ready for some deranged person to follow me through the door.

Then the guy from the parking lot appeared. But instead of raising an axe to kill us all, he stuck out his hand and said, "Hi, is this Mount Meadow Church? I'm Reverend Bill Pasture. Sorry I'm late. I had a hard time finding the place."

Look, I'm not the first person to mistake someone talking to himself as being up to no good. A priest named Eli saw this woman Hannah praying in the temple where he worked. She didn't look like she was praying so he thought she was just drunk and talking to herself.

"Stop getting drunk!" Eli said to her. "Throw away your wine!"

Hannah answered, "No, my lord, I have not drunk any wine. I'm just pouring out my heart to God because I don't know what else I can do."

Hannah really wanted to have a baby, and it just wasn't happening. So Eli prayed for her, and then she went home to her husband.

A while later, Hannah gave birth to a son, and she named him Samuel. When Samuel was old enough, Hannah took him back to the temple to meet Eli.

"Remember me?" she asked. "I was the woman you found crying and praying in the temple, and this is the son I prayed for. And now, because God heard my prayer and remembered me, I'm back to dedicate my son so that he will do God's work for as long as he lives."

Draw Here↓

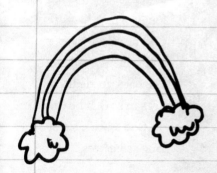

Who Needs a King?

1 Samuel 8-10

My mom always says I have a smart mouth, so I decided to put it to good use and join the debate team this year. The history teacher, Mr. Ledbetter, is our advisor. He did a pretty good job. He kept us from spending too much time talking about video games and gave us tips on how to win our matches.

But at one point, we got a little, well, full of ourselves and decided we didn't need his advice. We asked him, I guess more like *argued* with him, to let us choose our own leader. There are those smart mouths coming out again.

We finally wore him down and voted Jordan Lewis as our captain. I think he won because his mom has an E-Z screen-print T-shirt maker and she offered to make us all matching team shirts. Of course, that might not have been the best criteria to use to elect a leader. We lost our first debate  match. Actually, we got crushed. It was not pretty.

We're hoping that if we scrape all the gum off the desks in the history room we can talk Mr. Ledbetter into helping us again.

The Israelites decided they needed a different kind of ruler too. God had been leading them and gave them judges like Samuel to counsel them. But they demanded a king because they wanted to be like all the other nations. That's called giving in to peer pressure.

God told Samuel, "The people have rejected me from being their king. They are going to regret this."

God knew this was a big mistake, but He gave them a king anyway. He told Samuel how to find a man named Saul and told him to anoint Saul as king.

So Samuel poured oil over Saul's head and said, "I'm doing this so that everyone will know that you are God's choice to be the leader of His people. You'll rule over them and save them from their enemies."

Saul didn't do such a good job, just like God predicted. Luckily, Jordan Lewis wasn't nearly as bad as King Saul.

Saul is going to need some shampoo when this anointing is over.

YOU'VE GOT A SAFE PLACE IN THE PALACE FOR THIS BONE, RIGHT?

An Unlikely King

G od was sorry He had made Saul king over Israel and decided to give His people a new king.

God said to Samuel, "You're going to help me find a new king, but remember, I do not see the same way people do. People care about appearances, but I look at the heart."

With God's help, Samuel found a man named Jesse who had eight sons. Samuel met the seven oldest brothers first, but he saw that none of them was the next king.

"Are these all your sons?" he asked.

"No," said Jesse. "My youngest is out in the field taking care of the sheep."

Now in Bible times, baby brothers in large families didn't usually become kings. But when Samuel met this kid, God spoke to him.

"He is the one," God said to Samuel. "He is the next king."

David wouldn't reign for a while, not until after Saul died. He was still a kid, after all.

God took a baby brother—a lowly, harp-playing shepherd boy named David—and made him king. (Makes me glad I'm somebody's baby brother. Maybe I'll get to be prom king or something someday!)

"David, your family and your kingdom will last forever," God said (check out 2 Samuel 7:16).

David realized how much God loved him.

"Lord, I don't even know why you've been so good to me and my family. What more can I say to you? Lord God, you love me, your servant, so much!"

77

One Killer Shot

1 Samuel 17

I played baseball . . . once. As I've said before, I'm not very athletic and my baseball skills are lousy. And it didn't help that the pitcher was so big that his fastball could've broken my indestructible bat in two, or shattered my knocking knees, or crushed my nose. Come on, he was eleven and had a beard! I was so scared of the guy that I didn't even swing once.

Strike one! Strike two! Strike three!

I didn't mind striking out. I was grateful to still have my face.

King Saul and the army of Israel had to deal with a huge guy like that pitcher in the war against the Philistines. The dude was named Goliath. He was nine feet nine inches tall, and an expert in psyching out his opponents.

Goliath laughed at Israel's soldiers. I imagine he said something like, "Israel stinks and Saul's a dummy."

He dared Israel to send just one soldier to fight him. "Send out your best since you're such chickens!"

Even King Saul was afraid. But young David, who was now one of Saul's servants, stepped up to the plate. "I've got this, King. Send me out to slay this smelly jerk."

Even though Saul thought Goliath would eat the kid in one gulp, David convinced Saul to let him fight. David had a lot of faith in God, so he was confident that he had a major advantage over Goliath.

Goliath took one look at David and was disgusted that the Israelites had sent a kid to do a man's job. "Hey, shrimp, do you think I am a dog, that you come at me with a stick?" (Goliath used some pretty bad words to make fun of David here, but I can't really repeat those.) "I'll feed your body to the birds!"

But David said to him, "It doesn't matter how big you are or how many weapons you have. Next to God, you're tiny."

Goliath moved to attack David, and David ran to meet him.

He took a stone from his pouch. He put it into his sling and slung it. The stone bonked Goliath on the forehead, hard. The giant fell face-first on the ground. ◀━ **"God: 1. Goliath: DONE."**

So David defeated big bad Goliath with only a sling and a stone!

Now, I don't recommend that you throw rocks at the school bully tomorrow. But maybe a little faith in God will help you face whatever makes you scared.

Best Friends Forever

1 Samuel 18-20

I'm really lucky to have Austin as a best friend. Things with us have always been pretty simple, except for Penelope's Great Prom Incident. What I didn't tell you earlier was that Big A is the little brother of Big Bad Thad, the guy who had multiple prom dates and broke my sister's heart. Big A is nothing like his loser older brother, so it was easy for us to stay out of all of their high school drama. Things were never really weird for us, but it doesn't always work out that way for people related to bullies. Things got way complicated for David and Jonathan, the son of King Saul.

David and Jonathan were best friends.

After David's big victory over Goliath, he became really popular with the people of Israel. King Saul got crazy jealous and tried to kill David. More than once.

Jonathan's own father wanted his best friend dead. This made his friendship with David super difficult.

When the two friends finally got together to talk about what was going on, David told Jonathan about his father trying to kill him. They made a plan to find out if King Saul would admit his hatred for David to his own son. Not only did Saul admit he wanted to kill David, he threatened to kill Jonathan for being friends with David too. **That is not good parenting.** ⬅

Jonathan met up with David and told him David had to go away so that Saul couldn't kill him. They both cried—you probably would too if your best friend was moving and you would never see him again. But the two of them made promises to always care for the other's family no matter what happened.

Finally, Jonathan had to send David away for fear that Saul would catch up with them. "Go in peace, David," Jonathan said. "We've promised to always be friends, and with God's help, we always will be."

And then David and Jonathan went their separate ways.

You Just Got Solomoned!

1 Kings 3

Even though my sister, Penelope, is six years older than I am, we still fight on occasion. Especially about the remote. Dad got so sick of our fighting once when we were younger that he yelled at us—something he rarely does.

"If you kids don't stop, I'm going to pull a Solomon on you!"

Of course, we didn't know what he was talking about, so we ignored him and started chasing each other through the house with the remote.

Dad caught us in the hallway and took the television control. He told us that if we couldn't agree to share the remote then he was going to take it apart so that neither one of us could use it.

I was so mad I didn't care if I didn't get the remote, as long as Penelope didn't.

Penelope turned out to be a little smarter than I was, I am sorry to say, and realized that if he took it apart, we would have to get up to turn the TV on and off or change the channel. How awful would that be?! So she gave in and said I could man the remote.

When Dad handed *Penelope* the remote, he looked at me and said, "By the way, you just got 'Solomoned.'"

Totally uncool! I mean, she said I could have it.

Pen and I looked up Solomon in the Bible so we could understand what had just happened.

Solomon was King David's son. When David died, Solomon became the new king of Israel.

Like David, Solomon loved God and wanted to be a good king for God's people. One night God came to Solomon in a dream to ask him a question. "What can I give you to help you be a good king?"

"I can't do this without Your help," Solomon answered, "so give me wisdom to know right from wrong, to know good decisions from bad ones." I think Solomon was already pretty wise since he was smart enough to know he needed God's help to be a good ruler.

Not long after Solomon's dream, he had to make a decision that put his wisdom to the test.

Two women came before the king and both claimed to be the mother of the same child. There were no witnesses to ask who the real mother was and no DNA science to prove it. Solomon had to do something drastic to solve the mystery.

"Cut the baby in half," the king said.

"Fine," said one of the women, "go ahead and cut him in half."

But the other woman cried out, "No! Don't hurt him. She can have him."

Solomon knew that the woman who would rather give up the baby than hurt him was the real mother. And wise King Solomon was right.

They got Solomoned!

Never-Ending Miracle Bread

1 Kings 17

I love bread. Three kids in my class have to eat gluten-free food, which means they can't have regular bread—EVER. I can't imagine how horrible that would be. As far as I'm concerned, bread should have its own holiday.

The Bible tells a lot of stories about bread, especially about people not having any. One of the cooler bread stories is about a town called Zarephath and a widow and son who lived there. She was poor and had only a little bit of food left in her house. She didn't know how she would feed her kid once she ran out because there was a serious food and water shortage all over.

One day a stranger approached the widow and asked for some water.

She was going to the well in town to get some for him when the stranger asked for something more.

"Bring me some bread too."

Well, it was one thing to fetch a pail of water; it was something else to give the stranger food she couldn't even give her own son.

"God knows I don't have any bread to give you. I only have enough to give my son one last bite to eat before we starve to death."

But then the stranger, who was

> IT WOULD TAKE SOMETHING **PRETTY** WONDERFUL FROM GOD TO GET ME TO GIVE UP **MY** LAST BITS OF BREAD, AND I'M NOT EVEN STARVING!

actually a prophet named Elijah, told the widow that God had arranged their meeting and had something wonderful in store for her and her son. Elijah was one of the greatest prophets who ever lived. A prophet is someone who tells the truth about God and God's people, even when it's hard or gets them in trouble. It usually *does* get them in trouble, just FYI.

"Don't be afraid," Elijah said. "Just take what you have and make a little something for yourself, for your son, and for me. Then God will bless you with enough to eat."

The widow did what Elijah said because she believed. Turned out that no matter how much bread she baked, she always had enough supplies in her kitchen to make more, just like God said.

Mmmm, now that's a miracle I can sink my teeth into. I could use a tasty slice of never-ending miracle bread right about now myself.

Elijah's Hot Ride

2 Kings 2

My Grandpa Dave was pretty awesome. He smelled a little weird, but I loved hanging out with him. He was always telling crazy stories.

He talked about the war he fought in Vietnam, and he told what he called "cautionary tales" about criminals he arrested when he was a police officer. The moral to Grandpa's cautionary tales was basically: "If you're ever dumb enough to do whatever I'm telling you about, then you deserve to get arrested."

I know it's lame for a twelve-year-old to talk about how much he loved his grandfather, but I miss him. When he died last year, I don't think I have ever been that sad.

I don't know if the prophet Elijah was like a grandfather to Elisha, but they were definitely close. Elijah was also a great teacher, and his best student, a man named Elisha, was always with him.

MY MOM SAYS I GET MY STORYTELLING ABILITIES FROM GRANDPA.

Elisha hoped to be a prophet like Elijah someday, but he knew that he had a lot to learn. So wherever Elijah went, Elisha stuck close.

One day Elijah told Elisha that he had to go to Jericho and that Elisha shouldn't follow him. But Elisha refused to leave him.

So they hiked, and hiked, and crossed a river, and hiked some more.

Elijah finally stopped and asked Elisha, "What can I give you before I go?"

Elisha knew that meant it was time to step up and become a great prophet like his teacher. "I need twice as much of your help as you think I do."

"If you see what happens when I'm taken from you," Elijah replied, "then you'll get what you've asked for."

They talked for a while longer. Then suddenly, a chariot made of fire pulled by horses made of fire came out of nowhere and swooped up Elijah. The chariot took him higher and higher until he was out of sight, gone into heaven.

Despite the awesome exit, Elisha was still sad that Elijah had to go.

Biblical Zit Cure

2 Kings 5

When I turned twelve, and I mean the *day* I turned twelve, I received a very special gift. Pimples. Zits. Oozies. I call them a gift because they are the one thing that makes me look less like a little boy and more like an almost-teenager. I'm not a pizza face, so Mom won't let me get any of the superpowered, infomercial acne-clearing systems. So I just do a face patrol twice a day with basic drugstore pimple cream.

This guy named Naaman in the Bible needed *way* more than a little Clearasil for his skin disease. He was the commander of an army from Aram, a kingdom that often fought with Israel. Although he was very powerful and successful, nobody in Aram could help him get rid of his nasty skin disease. It was so bad that when the king of Aram heard there was someone in Israel who could help, he sent Naaman there with enough gold and silver to pay for skin treatment. Elisha, the prophet, stepped up to help Naaman.

When Naaman met Elisha, though, Elisha didn't ask for any money at all. In fact, he told the general to do something very simple.

"Go dip yourself in the Jordan River seven times," he said.

Naaman was furious. He was ready to pay for the best skin care money could buy. Now this crazy man was telling him to take a bath in a muddy river? "I don't *think* so."

WONDER IF THAT WILL HELP WITH MY WARTS?

But then one of Naaman's servants made a great point. "Sir, if he had told you to do something that was really difficult or really expensive, wouldn't you have done it? Why, then, won't you do this easy thing that the prophet has said?"

Naaman listened to his servant and did what Elisha said to do.

And guess what? After dipping himself in the water seven times, he was healed.

Naaman was so inspired by his miracle healing that he said, "I now know there is no God in all the earth except in Israel!" The powerful general went back to his country and worshipped God.

Maybe my mom will fly me to the Jordan River if my pimples get really bad . . .

The Most Impressive Girl Ever

The Book of Esther

R emember when I told you that our soccer coach had me on a mission to keep Big A away from girls during soccer season? Well, there is one girl I could never steer him away from. Her name is Abbie Paul, and she is possibly the most impressive girl alive.

Abbie is incredibly smart and really motivated. At the beginning of fifth grade, we found out the school board had cut music classes because of budget stuff.

On the second day of school, Abbie started a protest. She gathered every kid in the middle school who could sing or play an instrument. Just as the three-thirty bell rang, about 150 kids sat down in the hallway and played and sang "The Star-Spangled Banner."

No one would leave; they just kept playing the song over and over. Almost everyone missed their bus, and parents started calling the school wondering where their kids were.

Abbie got Principal Irvin to call a special meeting with the parents, students, and school board to figure out how to bring back the music classes. At the meeting, in front of, like, *the whole town*, Abbie explained her idea to ask each business in town to pay for two weeks of classes for that year.

She was amazing. And her plan worked. We got our music classes back that year, and we have them again this year.

I wrote her a note during math class to say thanks and told her she was like Queen Esther—a lady who got stuff done.

It was a pretty big compliment.

You see, Esther pulled off an impressive plan too. King Xerxes of Persia fell in love with Esther and made her his queen. But Esther had a secret plan. She was working to save her people—God's people.

The king really loved Esther. He loved her so much that he promised to give her anything she wanted.

That king is TOTALLY into his queen. TOTALLY.

"You could ask for half of my kingdom," he declared, "and I would give it to you."

Esther knew just what to ask him for. There were many harsh rules against God's people and she wanted to help them.

"If you love me," she said, "put an end to the laws that are hurting

me and my people. Let us live our lives the way we want to live them."

The king kept his promise. He protected Esther's people and punished the guys responsible for hurting them.

By the way, Abbie still has my note taped up in her locker.

Draw Here↓

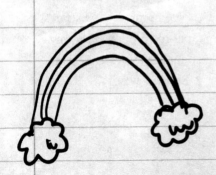

Things Could Always Get Worse

The Book of Job

Whenever my sister and I are having a bad day, week, or month and complain about it, my mom always says, "Just be thankful you aren't Job, dear. Things could always get worse." She thinks this will make us feel better, but it usually doesn't.

I mean, *really*. I don't think I will ever reach "Job Status." At least I hope not.

Job was kind of a big deal. He had a great family. He was rich. He had lots of friends. And most important, he loved God and did what was right in God's eyes.

Now, the devil wanted to make an example of Job to prove that his faith wasn't really that deep. Take away the good things in Job's life, the devil said, and he'll turn against God just like anybody else.

So God allowed Job's life to be turned upside down. He lost almost everything—his children, his land, all his stuff—and he got really sick too. Those who stuck around wondered why he didn't curse God for all the bad things happening in his life and die.

Woe is Job.

But Job never gave up on God. He had faith. Guess who did give up on Job?

Yep. The devil. In the end, God returned to Job all that he had lost and then some. That's the kind of faith I want to have—Job status or not.

This Is Not a Story About Zombies

Ezekiel 37

God had a job for Ezekiel. He needed Ezekiel to be a prophet. Prophets do lots of different things. They deliver messages from God to people. Sometimes they encourage people. Sometimes they challenge people. And sometimes they say and do things that are so strange that they confuse people. That's the kind of prophet God wanted Ezekiel to be—the confusing, weird kind.

God told him to eat a scroll (weird). God told him to preach (not weird) lying down (confusing). God even told him to cut off his hair and do some crazy stuff with it—and I'm not talking about a mohawk (very weird). And then God asked him to do one of the weirdest, strangest, creepiest things ever.

In a vision, God asked Ezekiel to preach a sermon to a pile of crusty old bones.

First, God showed Ezekiel the bones of a whole bunch of dead people. There were so many that they filled the valley where Ezekiel stood. There were bones all over the place. Then God asked Ezekiel a question: "Can these bones live?"

"Only You know, God," he said. ← **That was Ezekiel's way of saying that he had no clue what was going on.**

Then God told Ezekiel to tell the bones to live again.

Seriously, can you imagine telling dead bones to live again? Just try it the next time you finish a piece of fried chicken.

As far as Ezekiel knew, dead bones stayed dead, but he did what God asked him to do anyway. And when Ezekiel delivered the message that God had given him, something amazing happened. The old bones started to move, coming together to make whole skeletons. And the fun didn't stop there.

Tendons, muscles, and ligaments covered the bones, until bodies with skin and hair were all over the valley floor. But the bodies were still lifeless.

That's a tough crowd.

So God gave Ezekiel one more message to deliver. And when the prophet spoke it, the wind blew and the bodies came to life.

Then God told Ezekiel what he was looking at. "These are your neighbors, Ezekiel, the people of your country. They're ready to give up on themselves and on Me, but I'm not giving up on them. I will give them My spirit and a new life, and I will take you all home."

See! Not a story about zombies.

Daniel's Low-Carb Diet

Daniel 1

King Nebuchadnezzar (try saying that three times fast) defeated the king of the Israelites and took over their land. He was always up to no good. Have you ever met someone like that?

King Nebuchadnezzar was like that—always scheming. He was looking for a few good men he could train so he could make his kingdom even more powerful. He ordered his men to bring him some of the smartest, best-looking, most-ripped Israelites.

Daniel, Shadrach, Meshach, and Abednego were among the men chosen to serve in the king's top circle. These few were to be given food and wine from the king's table for three years while they were being trained. Can you imagine being brought into the king's chambers for a feast every day? Talk about diving into a mile-long table of Twinkies, pizza, Pop-Tarts, and slushies!

While many would have jumped at the chance to enjoy the king's food, Daniel and his friends refused to defile (which means mess up) their pure eating habits. The king's feasts probably included things like pork and other foods forbidden by Jewish law.

Daniel asked permission to eat according to God's laws, and assured the guards that they would be in much better shape than all of the other men if they did. One of the king's guards agreed to the test and secretly allowed Daniel and his three friends to eat only vegetables and water.

For ten days, the guard let the four bypass the king's table and eat pure foods. In those ten days, Daniel and his friends whipped up on the others in learning, strength, and their ability to understand visions and dreams, so the king promoted them above everyone else to serve in his kingdom.

By the way, the name Daniel means "judged by God." Makes sense since Daniel didn't cave in to the pressures surrounding him. Even if it meant death or torture, Daniel knew how to say no to people and yes to God.

Faith on Fire

Daniel 3

ebuchadnezzar became the greatest king in the world—but "great" in a bully kind of way. At Nebuchadnezzar's order, an idol (a fake god) was made. The idol was ninety feet tall and covered with gold.

They had access to some major bling, I guess.

The king ordered everyone in the kingdom to worship this blingy statue, and no one dared disobey. Head honchos everywhere fell to their knees—people like the mayor, the governor, and the school principal.

But three guys in the crowd—Shadrach, Meshach, and Abednego— refused to worship Nebuchadnezzar's latest, greatest gold god. Since they were leaders appointed by the king, everyone looked at them to see if they would kneel down when the king started playing his special "you'd better worship now" music. But they refused.

The king was furious. His face turned I-just-ate-a-jalapeño red in two seconds flat!

At his command, the king's soldiers tied up the three men with ropes and threw them into a furnace. They said, "Our God is able to save us from that furnace, but even if He doesn't, we will serve Him anyway."

The flames were so hot that they killed the soldiers who had shoved them in. But Shadrach, Meshach, and Abednego walked around in the middle of the flames unhurt!

Here's the craziest part. *A fourth person was in the furnace with them*—and that fourth person was the Son of God. The king's eyes must have widened to the size of my mom's favorite serving platter with the happy pilgrims and a freaked-out-looking turkey on it. He couldn't believe what he was seeing.

The king ran to the furnace door. "You servants of the most high God, come out! Come to me at once!"

They came out without a burn on them and didn't even smell like smoke! The ropes that bound them were the only things that had burned off.

The king declared the God of Shadrach, Meshach, and Abednego the one true God and decreed that everyone in the kingdom must worship their God.

That's our God too, btw.

Lion with Lockjaw

Daniel 6

Daniel wasn't your average Joe. Any kind of decree or law from the king wasn't going to change how he acted if it didn't line up with his beliefs.

He kind of reminds me of my friend Abbie Paul and her crusade to bring back music classes. Abbie could have gotten suspended from school—or worse, kicked out—for organizing the protest. But that didn't stop her from standing up for what was right. **(the most impressive girl alive)**

Stuff like that takes guts.

Imagine being face-to-face with a slobbering, hungry lion. Wait, we need to backtrack a little. How did Daniel get in this situation? Yup, you guessed it—he chose to follow God and do what was right instead of following the king's orders.

King Darius was now in charge, and he favored Daniel. Daniel was known for being super wise and an excellent leader. King Darius liked

Daniel and planned to give him authority over the whole kingdom.

But some other men thought they should be the ones in power, and they did *not* like Daniel. They followed him around and tried to catch him doing something wrong to keep him from getting promoted over them.

The only thing they could come up with was that Daniel prayed every day to God, so they went to King Darius and talked him into ordering everyone in the kingdom to stop praying for thirty days. The people could only ask the king for what they needed, and those who broke the law would be thrown to the lions.

What do you think happened? Daniel didn't obey the new law. His love for God and his desire to pray was more important than following the king's crazy law.

The officials ran back to the king and tattled on Daniel. With a heavy heart, the king ordered that Daniel be fed to the lions.

DANIEL IS THE LION WHISPERER.

Ugh. Can you imagine the lions circling Daniel and licking those gigantor sharp chops? I wonder what Daniel prayed.

My prayer would probably sound a little something like, "Dear Lord, any chance You could make me look like a plate of Brussels sprouts or lima beans? Anything but the pepperoni pizza (with a side of breadsticks) these lions think I look like . . . "

And then things got crazy. Um, crazi*er*.

Daniel must have said some powerful prayers because when King Darius called Daniel's name the next morning, Daniel answered, "May the king live forever. My God has sent an angel. The angel shut the lions' mouths, and they did not harm me. God knew I had done no wrong."

WHAT WE'VE GOT HERE ARE SOME FEROCIOUS- LOOKING LIONS . . .

Daniel walked out of that lions' den without a scratch.

Now, hold on to your yogurt. King Darius was so impressed with God's power and Daniel's faith that he ordered his soldiers to round up all the men who had schemed to get rid of Daniel and have *them* fed to the lions.

Yeah . . . and God didn't exactly see fit to deliver the bad guys. The lions got all the pepperoni pizza (with a side of breadsticks) they wanted that day!

The best part of all? The king ordered everyone to pray to Daniel's God, who had miraculously delivered him from certain death.

If Daniel went to our middle school, I bet he'd hang out with Abbie Paul. And once in a while, I bet they'd let me tag along.

And these guys → NEED a Lion Whisperer!

A Guy, a Fish, and a Very Bad City

The Book of Jonah

My mom has a sign in her kitchen that says, "Never look down on anyone . . . unless you are helping him up." That would have been a good sign for Jonah to have hanging in his tent. Because Jonah had a *tiny* problem judging others.

Okay, I'm not saying I've never judged someone or that I'm better than Jonah. When Mrs. Sarah Bellum, our science teacher, gives us back our grades for yet another pop quiz on the applications of superconduc- **You think I'm kidding about her name?** tors, I still don't get how some kids can get an F each and every time! It makes me want to pull my hair out. I mean, we went over it twice and watched a very well-produced Discovery Channel documentary on it. C'mon, people.

I am willing to admit that maybe I've got a little bit of Jonah judgment running through me.

See, God told Jonah to go to Nineveh: "Jonah, get up and go to Nineveh. Preach to the people, and warn them to turn from their wickedness."

Pretty clear, right?

But Jonah refused to go. Why? Because the people of Nineveh worshipped idols and did horrible things. Nineveh was a dangerous place. And who wants to hang out with—or help—wicked people?

So Jonah bought a one-way ticket on a boat going in the *opposite* direction of Nineveh. A one-way ticket to a future cage match with God! I mean, who goes up against God like that?

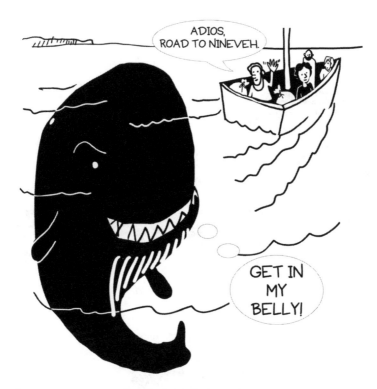

A storm came, and Jonah and the other sailors were terrified. They prayed, but the storm got worse. Jonah was pretty sure the storm might have something to do with him running away from Nineveh, so he told the others to throw him overboard to calm the storm.

"Heave-ho, there he goes!" And overboard Jonah went.

The seas calmed, and the crew thanked God.

But Jonah's day just got worse. A big fish, people often say a whale—*GULP!*—swallowed Jonah. For three days and three nights, Jonah lived inside the big fish . . . which means the mayor of Chumpville had plenty of time to pray.

God heard Jonah's prayer and caused the fish to vomit out Jonah and hurl him onto dry land. Gross.

God told him again to go to Ninevah, and this time Jonah went.

He preached the Word, and the people repented.

Draw Here!

Draw Here↓

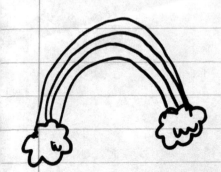

NEW TESTAMENT

It's a Boy!

Matthew 1; Luke 1

D o You ever watch super hero movies? Big A and I *love* to watch them. You know those parts where everyone is in big trouble? I mean, like, we're-all-gonna-die trouble? And then, *BAM*, the hero shows up and saves the day? Well, that's kind of what happened when God sent Jesus.

So the New Testament begins with the story of an angel named Gabriel visiting a young girl named Mary. He had big news for her—like the biggest news a girl could ever get—because Mary wasn't just any girl.

Mary was just minding her own business when an angel of the Lord shows up!

"The Lord is with you and you are greatly favored," Gabriel told her. He went on to tell her that she was going to have a child who would be—get this—the Son of God. Whoa.

Mary was beyond surprised because she was young and wasn't married yet.

But God took care of all of that for Mary. An angel also visited Joseph, who was Mary's fiancé, and told him to marry the girl who was "with child through the Holy Spirit."

Mary trusted God. She was filled with joy and knew her child would bless people everywhere.

Breakfast, Locusts Lunch, Locusts Dinner, Locusts

Matthew 3; Mark 1; Luke 1; John 1

So there was kind of a baby boom going on in Mary's family.

At the same time the angel Gabriel went to Mary with news that she would give birth to Jesus, he told her another world-changing piece of info: her cousin Elizabeth, who was *way* older than Mary, was also going to give birth to a baby, and his name would be John.

Of course, John wasn't just any baby. He had a big future in front of him as a prophet—one of the most important prophets in the Bible. God's main job for John (who became known as John the Baptist) was to tell everyone of Jesus' coming as the Messiah and the only One who could forgive the sins of humans.

Pretty big job, right?

John was super serious about prepping the world for his cousin Jesus.

I'll be honest about John. He probably didn't smell that great. I mean, he lived in the desert, and I'm guessing he didn't shower much. Oh, and the Bible says he kind of looked "wild." It also

> JOHN NEEDED A FASHION MAKEOVER.

says he ate dried locusts and wild honey. I prefer my honey without locusts, thank you very much!

In spite of his odd apparel, God used him to pave the way for Jesus and tell everyone the promised Messiah was coming.

The Perfect Baby, the Perfect Night

Luke 2

When my cousin Livvy Lu was born to my Uncle Mike and Aunt Tamara, we made pink cupcakes and bought pink blankets, pink hats, and pink socks the size of corn chips. By the end of that week, I was over pink.

But when Jesus was born, no one bought him a blue hat or a blue blanket or made him blue cupcakes.

Joseph and Mary lived in Nazareth, which was part of the Roman Empire. The Roman emperor commanded everyone to take part in a census in his or her hometown. I'm guessing that people needed to be counted so each town could update their population signs. People started traveling in different directions to obey the command.

A very pregnant Mary and her husband, Joseph, had to travel to Bethlehem, where Joseph had been born. Bethlehem was packed! Every hotel room, motel room, and bus station bench were filled. So they ended up in a stable outside of an inn. **They should have made a reservation.**

118

That very night, Jesus was born.

You might think God could have made better arrangements for His own Son's birth, right? Don't worry. God doesn't make mistakes. You see, a true king serves and sacrifices for people. He doesn't rule over them and live a life of luxury while others suffer. He comes in the place you'd least expect to find a king but in the place where He's most needed.

The stable was the perfect spot. For a perfect king. And everything that night was beautiful.

Some Shepherds Get a Miracle

Luke 2

The shepherds were hanging out with their flocks that night near Bethlehem. Suddenly, the angel of the Lord came to them to tell them the good news of Jesus' birth.

"Fear not," the angel said, "for, behold, I bring you good tidings of great joy, which shall be to all people. For unto you is born this day in the city of David a Saviour, which is Christ the Lord. Ye shall find the baby wrapped in swaddling clothes, lying in a manger."

Just wait. It gets better.

Then, even *more* angels appeared and broke out into an amazing chorus: "Glory to God in the highest and on earth peace, good will toward men" (KJV).

Can you imagine hanging out in a field with sheep all day and then suddenly being surrounded by angels singing the most amazing song you've ever heard? Jesus, the long-awaited Messiah, was here— and the angels dropped by to tell some lowly shepherds.

Kind of makes you want to be a shepherd, huh? Well, I Googled it—the last "true" shepherds live in the mountains of Serra de Estrela, Portugal. You wouldn't have running water, paved roads, cars, electricity, or Xbox, but hey, you just never know what miracle the day might hold.

Twinkle, Twinkle, Ginormous Star!

Matthew 2

I love to lay in my front yard at night and look at the stars. I can find the Big Dipper, Orion's Belt, and the Milky Way. Once in a while, I even see a shooting star. Sometimes Penelope comes out and looks up with me. We make up flavors for the stars. We pretend to take them out of the sky and eat them.

Sometimes we reach for the same star, which instantly creates a problem. It's usually the star one of us calls "warm glazed doughnut hole" that sends us into a full-blown wrestling match. Then Penelope pins me down and won't let me up until I eat dirt. This makes us both laugh so hard our stomachs hurt. Good times at the Wiley house.

There were people in the Bible who studied stars too (although they were probably way more professional and better behaved than Penelope and I are). After Jesus' birth, three of these guys who studied the stars noticed one star that was brighter than any other. It was huge—like the biggest-glazed-doughnut-hole-you've-ever-seen huge.

They knew this star was a sign from God that the Messiah, Jesus, had come to earth. So they followed that star until they found the Baby King.

Herod, an evil ruler at the time, heard about the wise men's preoccupation with the star and began to wonder if the "Savior" they spoke about would try to take Herod's throne. He told them to report back to him if they found the child . . . but God warned the wise men not to send a report, and they obeyed. Smart group.

Do you think they remembered the gift receipts? ↲

Once the wise men found Jesus, they were awestruck. They knew this was the Savior. They brought Him treasures, placed them in front of Him, and then bowed to worship Him.

The three wise men would never turn over the Savior to Herod. Instead, they warned Jesus' family to take Him somewhere safe so that Herod couldn't hurt Him (which really seems to me to be more common sense than wisdom, but "Three Common-Sense Men" doesn't have the same ring to it—you know?).

Draw Here↓

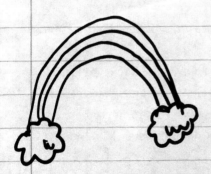

Missing: The Son of God

Luke 2

Sometimes it's hard for me to imagine Jesus as a kid, growing up and doing boy stuff just like me. Okay, maybe not *just* like me. I mean, He was the Son of God and all.

Well, one day Mary and Joseph sort of lost Jesus. I know, hard to imagine. My mom knows where I am ALL THE TIME. Seriously. It's like she has a tracking device embedded in my kicks or something. Mary and Joseph and the whole family had been to Jerusalem, where they celebrated the Passover feast every year. They were with a big crowd, so as they walked back to Nazareth, they assumed that Jesus was somewhere in the caravan of relatives. But when they stopped for the night, they couldn't find Him.

Mary and Joseph were worried. I mean, imagine how guilty you would feel if you lost the Son of God! So they headed back to Jerusalem to search for Jesus.

After three days, they finally found Him in the temple with the teachers, listening and asking questions.

When His mom asked Jesus why He had left them and stayed at the temple—scaring them to death, by the way—Jesus answered, "Why were you looking for Me? Didn't you know I would be at My Father's house?"

Even though they really didn't understand everything that was going on, Mary and Joseph knew that Jesus was God's Son. It was becoming clear to Mary—and probably everyone else—that Jesus wasn't just any kid. He was on a mission from God.

One time I got separated from my parents at the county fair, but unlike Jesus' mom and dad, mine pretty much knew where to look for me. We were apart for a grand total of six minutes. In that time, I had inhaled a huge ball of cotton candy, a funnel cake, and half a giant pickle—and then they found me. *Gulp.*

If Dad had found me at church listening to our pastor (instead of cramming my face with fair food), I probably wouldn't have gotten in nearly as much trouble or thrown up on the Spinerator later. Ugh.

Coming Soon: Jesus Christ

Matthew 3; Mark 1; Luke 3; John 1

R emember John? The locust-eating wild man? Well, he was growing up too, and he knew it was time to start telling everyone about the Messiah.

Both John and Jesus were so cool that it's no wonder they were related. They had guts—the cowboy–ninja–green beret kind of guts. If there was a battle, they didn't run. If there were haters around, they looked them straight in the eye! They stuck close to God, which explains the whole courage thing.

John left home and went throughout the hills of Judea preaching, "Repent! The kingdom of heaven is coming soon!" He was all about giving the coming Messiah—Jesus—His proper introduction. John was kinda like a movie poster in March announcing the latest summer blockbuster. Those posters get me totally psyched to sit in the dark with a jumbo bucket of popcorn and a box of Junior Mints. John the Baptist did the same thing—he got people psyched for Jesus.

The people got pretty excited because they were ready for the Messiah to come, like, now. They had been waiting a looooong time! And a lot of people who heard John's warning to stop sinning really did repent. Then he baptized them, which is how he got his name.

Some people thought John was the Christ, but the scruffy desert preacher didn't get a big head just because people loved his words and started following him around. He always pointed people's attention to Jesus.

John Baptizes Jesus

Matthew 3; Mark 1; Luke 3; John 1

Jesus was thirty years old when He left His home in Nazareth. He went to the Jordan River where John was preaching and baptizing people.

When John saw Jesus walking toward him, he got super excited and shouted, "This is the lamb of God who takes away the sin of the world. He is the One I have been telling you about, and He is much greater than I am."

Jesus told John to baptize Him, just like he was baptizing all those other folks. John wasn't sure that was such a good idea. He knew Jesus was God's son, and he didn't think he was the one who should be doing the baptizing here. But Jesus told him, "It's okay. This is part of God's plan." So John baptized Jesus.

When John brought Jesus out of the water, something crazy-awesome happened. The sky opened and the Spirit of God, in the form of a dove, came and filled Jesus! Then God's thundering voice spoke from heaven and said, "This is My beloved Son with whom I am well pleased."

Maybe it sounded sort of like the loudspeakers at school, but you wouldn't DARE talk during this amazing announcement.

This was the day that both John and Jesus had waited for. Remember, they were cousins, and they were both excited about the missions God had called them to.

I have a neighbor who says he's "called" to be a musician, and Mr. Kinnear says he's "called" to be our Sunday school teacher. Maybe God will call me to something important someday too? You can bet I'm looking out and listening for God to tell me.

Desert Showdown

Matthew 4; Mark 1; Luke 4

Just because we're kids, that doesn't mean we should walk around clueless about big, important things. We need to understand that there is a battle going on behind the scenes between good and evil, and although God has already won, the devil is still trying to put up a fight.

Jesus had just this kind of showdown with Satan. Right after He was baptized, Jesus headed out to the desert to fast and pray.

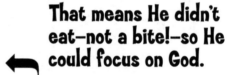

That means He didn't eat—not a bite!—so He could focus on God.

After forty days, when Jesus' body was really weak, Satan came to tempt Him. The enemy tried to get Jesus to do things to "prove" He was the Son of God. Satan even tried to get Jesus to follow him instead of God.

Yeah, right. Like that was going to happen.

He tempted Jesus with food, fame, and the power to rule over a million or so kingdoms.

But Jesus was tough and did not give in. Every time the devil opened his slippery, snaky mouth—*bam!*—Jesus hit him with a scripture! Jesus believed 100 percent that God would give Him the

I have trouble saying no to a candy bar. Jesus had nerves of steel!

strength and wisdom He needed to make that devil go away, and He did! Ultimately, the devil scrammed like a roach when the light hits it, and angels came to take care of Jesus.

He Didn't Even Need Bait

Matthew 4; Mark 1; John 1

John the Baptist was busy talking about the Messiah and telling people all the things they were doing that were against God's Word. That upset King Herod, who didn't much like being told he did anything wrong, so he put John in prison. After that, Jesus returned to Galilee and lived in Capernaum. He was walking along the Sea of Galilee one day when He saw two brothers—Simon, whom Jesus later renamed Peter, and Andrew—fishing in the lake.

Here comes one of the best lines in the New Testament: "Come, follow Me," Jesus said to the two. "I will make you fishers of men." ⬅ **That was probably the weirdest job offer they'd ever gotten.**

Penelope is great as far as big sisters go, but she's seriously addicted to practical jokes. When I was four, I came home from my Lil' Bits Sunday school class with that Bible verse on my coloring sheet. Penelope lovingly propped me up on her knee and told me in great detail about the meaning of the verse.

She told me all about Manonahook Lake in northern Wyoming, where you can use Oreo cookies as bait and fish for real men just like the Bible said. My mom took a picture of me gazing at Penelope like she was Batman telling me about his secret lair.

When Penelope retells the story (which she does about a zillion times a year), I say, "Bravo, Pen, you pulled one over on a four-year-old."

But back to Jesus and His disciples.

I am not sure if they really knew what Jesus was talking about. But the Bible says that when Jesus called to them, they immediately stopped what they were doing and followed Him. They must have sensed that they would be going on an awesome adventure with the best fisherman there ever was.

Which is way better than skinning stinky fish all day, right?

Jesus & Co.

Matthew 4; 10; Mark 1; Luke 5-6; John 1

After Peter and Andrew, Jesus called ten other men to follow Him: John, Philip, Nathaniel, Bartholomew, Matthew, Thomas, James, Simon, Thaddeus (the book of Luke calls this disciple Jude), and Judas Iscariot. How cool would that be, to go around with a band of brothers all the time?

For three years, these guys were inseparable and grew to love Jesus and each other. They were buds, friends forever. They traveled together, shared meals, prayed, studied Scriptures, and witnessed as Jesus taught. They helped people, healed them, and performed miracles in cities and throughout the countryside.

Textbook definition of ~~quantity,~~ er, QUALITY time.

I have a group of friends I trust too. They aren't perfect, and sometimes we annoy each other, but all in all, they are pretty good guys—that is, when we aren't competing to see who can eat a whole pizza the fastest. That never ends well . . .

Put Your Lamp (and Tap Shoes) on a Stand

Matthew 5; Luke 8

I like to tap dance. There, I said it. When I was three, I started taking tap lessons. Mom said we needed to "run some of the fun" right out of me because getting me to take a nap was like lassoing a bumblebee.

Turns out, I'm pretty good at tap.

But I wasn't always proud of that. I actually hid it from just about everyone. The day after I won the state championship for the eight-and-under Tap Champs, my picture was on the front page of the paper. As soon as I saw my big old face plastered right there for everyone and their dog to see, I headed out the back door, jumped on my bike, and scooped up as many newspapers around the neighborhood as I could carry. I guess hiding twenty-seven papers isn't exactly the perfect cover-up. The word got out anyway. But guess what? A lot of people actually thought it was cool. Sure, I got teased by some kids who called me "happy feet" and "twinkle toes," but a bunch of others patted me on the back and gave me high-fives. I still tap dance, and I even inspired a few kids at school to try it. And . . . it just so happens that tap dancing sets me up to be potentially the most multitalented hip-hop dancer ever.

Jesus said we are supposed to stand out and shine. In Matthew 5:14–15, He said, "You are the light that gives light to the world. A city that is built on a hill cannot be hidden. And people don't hide light under a bowl. They put it on a lampstand so the light shines for all the people in the house."

Jesus wanted us to be excited about being His followers and to share the awesome news of God's love. If we know God and don't tell others about Him, then our light is hidden . . . and that means God is hidden from people who need Him. And when God gives you a special talent, you need to show that to everyone too.

I get why people are afraid to show their light. Maybe they're worried they'll get made fun of. Maybe they don't want to be different from everyone else. Or maybe they're afraid they'll lose friends.

Being afraid of standing up for who you are as a Christian and sharing all the good stuff God has done for you will only bum you out. Truth is, I like tap dancing. It makes me feel good, and it's really, really hard work—just like any other sport. When I was hiding my love of tap, it kind of took some of the fun out of it. But once everyone knew, I was able to stop worrying, the people I really cared about were there to cheer me on.

Putting a light under a basket is a fire hazard too.

So I guess it's settled. I will put my light (my faith) on a stand (out in public) and stop trying to hide it. And I will tap dance till my toes fall off . . . or until Mom calls me down for dinner.

Hey, don't judge. It's taco night!

The Trouble With Sandcastles

Matthew 7; Luke 6

My dad has a lot of talents, but building things, especially bigger-than-a-birdhouse structures, just ain't one of 'em. Still, everyone in our family gave him an A for effort last year when he and I set out to build a tree house together. Our neighbor sat on his back porch every day, watching and shaking his head as the series of unfortunate events unfolded. Once in a while he'd yell out, "You know you oughta . . ." But then he'd catch himself and go back to sipping his iced tea, muttering to himself.

See, my dad was convinced he could build the tree house without any instructions. "How hard can it be?" he kept saying. "It's a tree house!" So he guesstimated the measurements, and every time my mom suggested drawing it out on paper, he'd tap his finger on his temple and say, "It's all in here, honey. It's. All. In. Here."

My dad's the best, but I think after all was said and done, each one of us agreed—even Dad—that the treehouse looked like a few boards and a rope had fallen from the sky and accidentally landed in our backyard oak.

In Matthew 7:24, Jesus told His followers to be "wise builders." This is one of those Bible stories that is pretty easy to understand. He said that if you hear His words and actually *follow them*, you are wise—like the guy who built his house on a rock. When the rains came, his house survived the storms. But if you hear His words and *don't follow them*, you are just plain dumb—like the dude who built his house on the sand. The first rainstorm totally obliterated his house and washed it right off the beach.

Location, location, location.

It took me a little while to figure out that this story from Jesus isn't actually about building houses at all. I think maybe sometimes I get bored at church because I hear what's being said, but I don't *do* anything with what I learn. That's what you call a house built on sand.

This week our pastor said something about forgiving others. I've been mad at Adam Zapple since he told Abbie Paul that I had head lice.

So I've decided it's time to forgive him.

I forgive you, Adam. Especially since you came down with head lice **AND** chicken pox in the same week. No one deserves that, dude!

Draw Here!

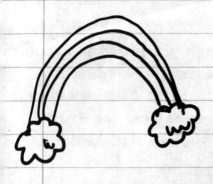

143

Faith Comes Through the Rooftop
Matthew 9; Mark 2; Luke 5

One time I gave up my window seat on the bus—a seat I'd had for *three years*—so that my best friend Austin could sit next to Vanessa, the girl he has a crush on. In silence. It's no coincidence that Austin went home that day and renamed the family dog Vanessa, even though his name had been Rambo for the past six years. I'm not sure Vanessa would be impressed that there's now a dog named after her, but yeah, Big A had it bad. Real bad.

Anyway, giving up my window seat on the bus is nothing compared to what four friends did for their paralyzed friend.

By now everyone knew that Jesus was wise, kind, and had the power to heal. So people followed Him everywhere He went. One day in Capernaum, a bunch of people crammed into the house where Jesus was staying. Friends, skeptics, lookie loos, and people who were sick gathered around until the place was packed.

Then the crowd heard some noise on the roof. Suddenly a group of four men carved a hole in the roof and started lowering their friend down on a mat through the hole.

The room got really quiet. "Uh, does anyone see what I'm seeing?" one guy probably whispered. Everyone wondered what Jesus would do.

Jesus looked at the man and said, "Be happy! Your sins are forgiven!"

The scribes and Pharisees who had come to find fault with Jesus thought awful things when they saw Him healing hurt people. But Jesus could hear the thoughts in their hearts. This is where He really freaked them out. "Why are you thinking like this?" He said. "Is it

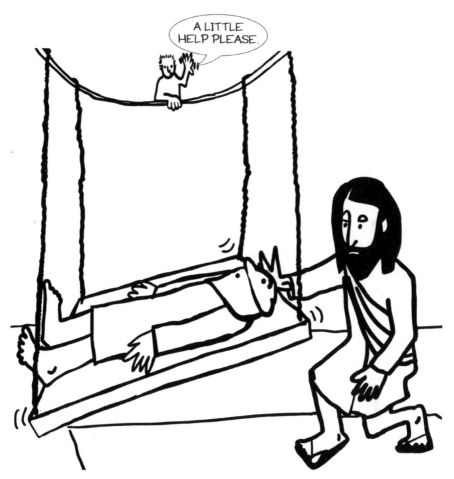

easier for me to tell this man, 'Your sins are forgiven,' or to say, 'Stand up and walk'? You will see that I have the power to do both."

Jesus said to the paralyzed man, "Stand up, take your mat, and walk home."

The man got up and began to walk! Can you imagine? Everyone was beyond amazed. They saw Jesus do two super cool things: He forgave the man of his sins, and He healed him.

The other thing I like about this story is that the four friends risked everything to get their friend healed. They cut a hole in someone else's roof. That's a serious buddy bond!

I bet the crowd went a little wild as the *five* friends walked away!

Storm Chaser

Matthew 8; Mark 4; Luke 8

One time I went deep-sea fishing with my dad. I thought it was going to be this great adventure. Big A went once with his dad, and he caught a small hammerhead shark. How cool is that? I could see myself reeling in one of those suckers! There was just one little problem: I didn't know that I get really seasick. I won't give you the gory details, but let's just say that I spent most of the day either lying on the smelly boat floor, groaning in agony, or hanging over the back of the boat.

As the day went on, the water got really choppy and rocked the boat even more. I was too sick to be scared, but I can understand why the disciples freaked out when they got stuck out on the sea in the middle of a storm.

Jesus had spent the whole day teaching the people by the Sea of Galilee. When night came, Jesus said, "Let's cross over to the other side of the lake." So Jesus and His disciples climbed into a boat. Since Jesus was exhausted, He went to the back of the boat and fell asleep.

Suddenly, a storm hit.

Waves crashed, and water began to flood the boat. The disciples were terrified, positive they were going to sink. "How can Jesus sleep through this storm?" they wondered.

"Wake up!" they cried. "Lord, save us!" According to Mark, the disciples asked Jesus, "Teacher, don't You care that we are going to drown?"

Jesus woke up and looked at them. "Why are you afraid?" He asked. "Don't you have any faith?"

Jesus stood up, raised His arms, and commanded the wind and waves to s-t-o-p. And immediately everything was calm.

The disciples were amazed. They must have looked at Jesus like He was a superhero. "Who is this," they asked, "that even the wind and the sea obey Him?"

I'm pretty sure their faith in Jesus skyrocketed that day.

I think calming the storm was easier than calming the disciples.

Also Not a Story About Zombies

Matthew 9; Mark 5; Luke 8

Some people are what you call skeptics. They don't believe anything until you prove it to them a million times. Like my science teacher, Ms. Sarah Bellum. We can tell her that it's storming outside, but until she sees her car float past the classroom window, she will not go roll up her windows on her car. Even then, she checks the weather app on her phone to make sure we aren't pulling a fast one on her.

That's how some people acted toward Jesus when He was teaching in Capernaum.

Jairus, a synagogue ruler, had sought out Jesus that day to ask Him to heal his sick daughter. As Jairus patiently waited for his turn to speak to Jesus, Jairus's friends told him, "Jairus, your daughter is dead. Why bother Jesus anymore?"

Ignoring them, Jesus told Jairus, "Don't be afraid. Just believe."

Taking a few disciples, Jesus went to Jairus's home. When they arrived, people were crying and wailing. Back then, loud crying was considered a sign of respect for the dead and their families. People even hired "professional mourners" (weird, huh?) to publicly grieve.

Jesus told the people to stop crying. "The girl isn't dead. She's sleeping."

My mom cries at about every movie. I bet she could have made some big bucks being a professional wailer back then.

The wailers laughed in Jesus' face. But their laughs didn't faze Him. He walked past them and went into the house. Jesus took the girl by the hand and said, "Little girl, I say to you, get up!"

HEY! WHAT'S FOR DINNER?

Get this: *the girl got up.* Which means the people probably had to shut their wailing mouths. Jesus then told them to give her something to eat. Jesus had totally brought her back from the dead and cured her—and she wasn't a zombie. Pretty cool, huh?

This is the point where Ms. Bellum would have gotten out a stethoscope to check the girl's heartbeat. I guess there will always be doubters, but if I had seen that little girl dead and then get up and eat a fish sandwich, I would believe Jesus could do anything!

Healing Party at the Bethesda Pool

John 5

Last summer, at Wild Waters Fun Park, I finally conquered one of my biggest fears: the Zoomerang. I've avoided the Zoomerang since I was five, but I decided I was going to *own* that oversized, death-defying, fiberglass faucet! This isn't just any waterslide. The Zoomerang is as high as the Empire State Building and has more twists and turns than a plate of spaghetti. I've heard you have to duct tape your hair down because the sheer velocity of the Zoomerang will peel it right off.

And to make the whole thing more intense, if you were the first person down the slide when the park opened, people said the ride was even faster. I didn't know if that was true or not, but I figured if I was going to try it, I might as well go big. So I talked my mom into taking us before the park even opened, and me and my buddies waited in line so that I could be the first one down.

Well, I made it down the Zoomerang.

Once.

I don't remember much about it, but Abbie Paul, who was there with her youth group, saw me hit the exit pool (Austin says he clocked me at about 106

LOOK AWAY!
I AM
NOT
CRYING!

mph). When I didn't come up right away, she jumped the line and dove in. Everyone said she looked like a real life guard the way she pulled me out of the water. My mom thinks I must have gotten dizzy from the "excitement" of the Zoomerang. My friends say it came to life and tried to kill me.

I thought about that experience at the Wild Waters Fun Park when I read about the pool at Bethesda. People thought that if you were the first person who stepped into the water when it started moving, it could heal you, so there were lots of people waiting to get in.

One morning, Jesus walked beside the pool. A crippled man who had not walked for years was sitting on a mat near the water's edge. Jesus asked him, "Do you want to be made well?"

The man told Jesus that there was no one to carry him to the water in time to be healed.

Jesus replied, "Take your bed and walk."

What do you think happened? That man got up, picked up his mat, and *walked*. Jesus had healed him!

That's a much better ending to a story than mine. Getting healed by Jesus beats getting rescued from a water slide any day.

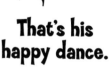

That's his happy dance.

A+ in Holy Math

Matthew 14; Mark 6; Luke 9; John 6

Science and art are my favorite subjects. But math? Well, all those digits just dance right past me. Sometimes I even think I see the number 8 looking up at me and making faces. But if you give me holy math, I pretty much get an A+. You see, it's a simple equation: Jesus + Anything = Miracle. It's the same every time—you don't have to run any equations or memorize any crazy formulas.

Holy math is what Jesus used one day when He just had seven loaves of bread, a few fish, and a crowd of four thousand to feed. The Bible says that's just how many men there were. That number doesn't include the women and children, so we are talking lots of people!

People came from all over to hear Jesus preach in the countryside. They brought the blind, deaf, crippled, and sick to Him to be healed. And He healed them.

On the third evening, Jesus could feel all the needs of those who were listening to Him and following Him, and He was filled with compassion. He told His disciples they needed to feed the crowds, who would soon be heading home. But they were out in the middle of nowhere, and all they had were seven small loaves of bread and a few fish.

Fortunately for them, as long Jesus is with you, things are going to be A-OKAY.

Jesus told the people to sit down. He blessed the seven loaves and a few fish. Then He fed *every single person* from the boy's lunch. And there were seven baskets of food leftover!

Now that's some math I can get my head around!

It's that "holy math" I was talking about—comes right after calculus.

Kids Rock

Matthew 19; Mark 10; Luke 18

Last year an accountant named Mr. Higgins came to our house. Mom and Dad were meeting with him about doing their income taxes. My cousin Livvy Lu, who was only about a year old and still considered a nonlethal weapon, was at our house. She was just starting to walk, and for some reason she became obsessed with trying to climb up into Mr. Higgins's lap. Mom kept giving me the eye, and I got the message that it was my job to distract Livvy Lu. But no matter what I did—and I am a master at making faces and playing peek-a-boo—she would squirm away from me and stumble back over to Mr. Higgins.

Mr. Higgins was not amused.

Now, I am not a baby person, but even I found it hard to resist Livvy Lu when she gave me that snaggled tooth smile and wanted to give me a big sloppy kiss.

Mom and Dad ended up hiring another accountant. When I asked why, Mom said, "Never trust a person who ignores a baby." Then she laughed and said she was just kidding.

But I thought Mom might have a point. Kind of like Jesus and the little children in the gospels.

The disciples kept getting all bent out of shape because parents would bring their children to Jesus to have Him bless them. But Jesus told the disciples to calm down. "Let the little children come see Me. Don't keep them away. God's kingdom belongs to them." He also told the disciples that everyone should have faith like little children.

The disciples made the mistake of thinking that Jesus' time was too important for kids. But Jesus flipped that right on its head!

Jesus loves kids. He knows kids just believe and trust. It's simple. That's the kind of faith He wants us *all* to have.

I bet Jesus loves even pesky little brothers and sisters too.

Consider Your Mind Blown

Matthew 5-7; Luke 6

I don't know about you, but it seems to me that a lot of the most powerful people in the world aren't always the nicest. I watch the news with my dad sometimes and I get the feeling being nice and gentle aren't always the most important qualities to have if you want to be successful. Jesus often taught the *opposite* of what the world believes, and it really blew everybody's minds. In the famous Sermon on the Mount, Jesus told the people about another way to live, a way that was better and that would be blessed by God. Here's where He said:

I've put a few of my own notes in as well. ↓

"Blessed are the poor in spirit (**those who don't brag, show off, or get grabby**), for theirs is the kingdom of heaven."

"Blessed are they who mourn (**those who are sad, cry, or fail big time**), for they shall be comforted."

"Blessed are the meek (**those who are gentle, patient, humble**), for they shall inherit the earth."

"Blessed are they who hunger and thirst for righteousness (**those who are fair and seek God**), for they shall be satisfied."

"Blessed are the merciful (**those who help and forgive others**), for they shall obtain mercy."

"Blessed are the pure of heart (**those who are honest and kind**), for they shall see God."

"Blessed are the peacemakers (**those who are non-fighters, cool under pressure, friendly**), for they shall be called children of God."
"Blessed are they who are persecuted for the sake of righteousness (**made fun of for their faith**), for theirs is the kingdom of heaven."

I can get pretty discouraged sometimes when the mean kids seem to always get their way. But Jesus said that if we try to be more like Him, and live the way God wants us to, then we will be blessed. And I will take God's blessings over the world's any day.

Draw Here↓

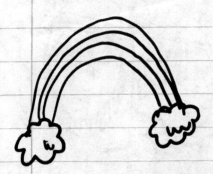

Jesus Walks on Water? Rad!

Matthew 14; Mark 6; John 6

For my birthday this year, our family went to see The Amazing Cosmo. He's a famous illusionist. He does this cool thing at the end of his show where he flies across the room, over everyone's heads. The entire crowd gasps or screams, especially the little kids. They still think that Aladdin gets around on a magic carpet and Superman can really reroute a Boeing 747 with his bare hands.

← When I got home, I looked up Cosmo's flying trick on YouTube. Pretty impressive with the physics, Cosmo!

But I know better. I know tricks are optical illusions.

When God does something unbelievable and beyond human understanding, though, you can bet it's no illusion; it's a miracle. And let me tell you, this next one is gonna blow your mind. I can guarantee you won't find a how-to video about it.

After a long day of teaching the crowds, Jesus told the disciples to get in their boat and sail to Capernaum, sent the crowds away, and went up alone on a mountain to pray. During the night, a huge storm blew across the sea and began to whip against the tiny boat. Soon, the waves were bigger than the boat, and things weren't looking so hot for the disciples. I bet they were thinking, *Man, of all the times to be without Jesus, this is* not *the night!*

Jesus knew the disciples were on the water and needed Him. So

He *walked across the water* toward the boat. The disciples didn't recognize Jesus at first and freaked out. ←**Of course they freaked out!**

"Hey, guys. It's Me, Jesus. Don't be scared," Jesus said.

On a scale of one to ten, this miracle was, like, a *thirteen*. No wonder they were afraid. It had to have been pretty spooky, seeing someone walking toward them (did I mention ON THE WATER?!) in the middle of the storm.

While the rest of the disciples were still rubbing their eyes, trying to comprehend that it was actually Jesus out there, Peter yelled to Jesus, "Lord, if that's You, tell me to come out to You and I'll walk on the water too."

So Jesus said, "Come on then, Pete."

Peter got out of the boat and walked toward Jesus—*on top of* the water!

Suddenly, a strong wind came. Peter got scared and began to sink.

"Oh, Peter," Jesus said. "What little faith! Why don't you trust Me?" Jesus reached out His hand to save Peter, and together they climbed into the boat.

Can you imagine if I up and walked on water across the public pool, looking for my goggles on the other side? People would freak out!

I bet the disciples had a new understanding of the kind of power Jesus had after that. They got to see some pretty amazing stuff! And the best part is that God does miracles not to impress us, but to show us how much He loves us.

Fishy Money

Matthew 17

I saved up my lawn-mowing money—$15 smackers—so I could buy a $14.99 snow cone machine. A penny to spare! But when I got to the register, the total was $16.38. *Whaaaaaat?*

I looked at my mom, who muttered, "Taxes." She covered the extra and told me that taxes paid for the roads we drove on to get to the store to buy that snow cone machine. I asked her if we could hang glide to the store next time and not pay the tax. She laughed and said taxes pay for the things we all use—roads, water pipes, streetlights, firefighters' salaries, police cars—things we probably don't think about much.

When Jesus and His disciples arrived in Capernaum, the tax collectors approached Peter and asked, "Doesn't your teacher pay the temple tax?" Peter answered yes.

Later Jesus talked to Peter about the tax issue. He helped Peter understand that kings and their families didn't pay taxes; the people they ruled did. Jesus and the disciples were like the king and his family. But even though they didn't have to pay taxes, they did because they didn't want to offend the people.

Even though they technically didn't have to. ⬅

Then Jesus told Peter to go to the lake and throw out his fishing line. The first fish Peter caught would have enough money in its mouth to pay the taxes that were due.

Jesus was willing to follow the rules of men so that His message of salvation would be received with open hearts and minds.

Now that's a real king—wise, humble, and a taxpayer, like the rest of us. Next time I guess I will save a little extra to pay the taxes (or go fishing before I head to the store), and I will try not to grumble so much about it.

The Good Samaritan...
and Penelope's
Best Date Ever

Luke 10

Remember Penelope's "prom incident" (getting jilted by Big Bad Thad)? I guess God had a plan with that whole heartbreak for Pen because after that she became, like, 2% nicer to just about everyone, including me.

Anyway, when Homecoming came around in the fall, Penelope surprised us all and asked Ryan Kinderman to go with her. Ryan is one of the more popular kids at Pen's school. He's the water boy for the football team, the vice president of the theater club, and does the morning announcements. He's super involved and everyone loves him, but Ryan has never had a date. He always gets, well, passed by. That's because he looks and acts a little different. Ryan has Down syndrome, which is a condition that affects mental and physical development.

Pen could see that Ryan was sad about not having a Homecoming date. He was standing at the sign-up table, his hands dug deep in his pockets and his head hanging down. Anyway, instead of just feeling sorry for him, Penelope did something about it. She got down on one knee in front of everyone and asked Ryan to be her date!

Ryan looked great in his tux, and Penelope? Well, I admit—for a dress, it wasn't terrible. They got matching corsages and ate at a fancy restaurant. Penelope said it was her best date ever. And she got everyone, including me, looking around and seeing who we might reach out to—instead of passing by them.

It makes me think about the story Jesus told about the Good Samaritan.

One day, robbers attached a Jewish man traveling along the old Jericho Road. They took his clothes and money, beat him up really, really badly, and left him half dead. First, a priest passed by. Then a Levite man kept on a-walkin'.

Then a Samaritan man came along, but he did something totally different.

Both of the religious guys looked down at the dying man and actually CROSSED THE STREET and walked on the other side!

First of all, The Samaritan *stopped*, and then he bandaged the man's wounds, and with great care placed him on his donkey. He took the wounded man to a nearby inn and paid the innkeeper to take care of the man up to two months.

And this was kind of a big deal because ➥ **Jews and Samaritans weren't exactly BFFs.**

As Jesus was telling this story, He asked, "Which of these three men was a neighbor to the one who was attacked by robbers?"

"The man who treated him kindly," a lawyer who had been challenging Jesus answered.

"Then go and do the same," Jesus said.

Being a good neighbor doesn't mean being nice only to your actual neighbors—or even people just like you. It means being kind and caring to everyone in need—regardless of any differences you might have.

The Prodigal Son Gets a Party

Luke 15

It has taken me a really long time to understand the story of the prodigal son. You know the one. Some smart-aleck trouble-maker kid asks for his inheritance *before* his dad has even died (can you imagine saying that to your dad?!?), leaves home, spends all the cash, works on a farm, gets so hungry he wishes he could be eating slop with the pigs, and finally heads home broke and filthy.

And when he comes home, his dad throws that kid a *HUGE party*.

Kinda makes me want to be run away from home sometimes. But my mom is quick to remind me: "Remember that time you ran away when you were five? You were so scared you only made it next door." I didn't get a party when I got home either.

Who wants a big bowl of pig slop?

Here's the thing. I guess you have to look at the *whole story* of the prodigal son before you go off and dream of being one. Let's take a look at the rest of what happened.

So we already know the basics of what the younger son did. When the partying and fun were way over, the son headed for home in shame. When the father recognized the filthy guy dressed in rags coming toward his house, the father ran and threw his arms around the boy. He was overjoyed that his son was alive. He ordered that the fanciest clothes and best food be prepared to celebrate his son's homecoming. There might have even been a piñata. And a bouncy castle.

Here's the part that makes *total sense* to me: the older son was really mad! If I went off and spent the family inheritance and left Penelope at home to do chores for years, she probably wouldn't be real happy to see me. The older brother pouted and wouldn't join the party. He had served his dad faithfully, hadn't wasted the money, and the father hadn't even given him a goat to celebrate with his friends!

YOU KNOW THAT'S WHAT I ALWAYS ASK FOR IF I'VE BEEN ON MY BEST BEHAVIOR: A GOAT. SO MY FRIENDS AND I CAN HAVE A PARTY.

But the father gently reminded the older son that everything the father had already belonged to the older son, but they should still celebrate the return of the younger son because he had turned from his ways and come back to them. "He was lost. Now he is found. He was dead and he is alive again."

Mom helped me understand what Jesus was teaching with this story—God's forgiveness of our sin and His unconditional love for us. Of course, God wants us to follow Him. But if we do run off like that younger son, doing whatever we want, He still watches from the driveway, anxious for our return *no matter what*, ready to throw a party that we've returned to Him. God loves us so much that He only cares that we are *found*, even if we mess up big time. And He honors and loves us just as much when we stick close, loving Him and serving Him—in fact, everything He has is ours!

Draw Here↓

A Short Guy Gets a Second Chance

Luke 19

Zacchaeus was a tax collector and wasn't exactly the most popular guy. But when he found out that Jesus was coming to town, he got really excited. Everybody had been talking about Jesus and wanted to see who this guy was. Including Zacchaeus.

There was just one problem. The crowd was huge, and Zacchaeus? Well, he was super short. Like Keebler Elf short.

What's a short guy to do in a situation like this? Go climb a tree—duh. I happen to have some experience in this department. Apparently Zacchaeus had some experience with tree climbing too. He found a sycamore tree, climbed that thing, and had the best seat in the house.

← Sometimes I climb the oak in our front yard so I can spy on Pen when her dates come to pick her up.

As Jesus walked along the road with His disciples, the people waited eagerly to catch a glimpse of Him. Jesus stopped right under a sycamore tree next to the road. He looked up, and there was Zacchaeus, peeking down through the branches.

"Zacchaeus!" Jesus said. "Hurry down from there! I'm staying at your house today!"

I can imagine Little Z looking back and forth at the crowd. "You talkin' to me?" No one was more shocked at Jesus' attention than Zacchaeus. He flew down that tree quicker than a monkey chasing a running banana. When his feet hit the ground, he was so happy he could have danced a jig. Together Jesus and Zacchaeus started off toward Zacchaeus's house.

But the people in the crowd grumbled and mumbled about the tax collector they considered a pesky crook. They had spent all day in the hot sun following Jesus, and now He was going to stay at the house of a rich, cheating tax collector?

But Zacchaeus's heart was changed by Jesus' kindness. "Listen! I will give half of everything I have to the poor! And if I cheated anyone, I will pay them back four times as much!"

Jesus always knows what He's doing. He knew that out of everyone in that crowd, the swindling tax collector was *exactly* who He should be spending extra time with. Jesus said to Zacchaeus, "Today salvation has come to this house. That's why I am here. I came to find and save the lost!"

Zacchaeus was a short dude, but on this special day, Jesus made him feel ten feet tall.

A Mighty Mite

Mark 12; Luke 21

When Mr. Kinnear started talking about "the widow's mite" at youth group one night, I confess: I started itching. Like, all over. Just the word *mite* made me think of termites or fleas or mosquitos or some kind of creepy-crawly critters with three thousand legs.

Anything over eight legs is too ← many.

In this story, it turns out a mite was *not* a flesh-devouring bug. It was a kind of coin not worth very much. Even less than a penny. I'm twelve and all I ever really have is a mite. I'm not exactly turning into Donald Trump with the lawn-mowing gigs.

The Bible says that one day Jesus went to the temple and sat near where the offerings were placed. He watched the people as they came by and put in their offerings. Many rich people, dressed in fine robes,

came by and put in a lot of money. But then a poor widow came by and put in two small copper coins (*mites*) that together weren't even worth a penny.

Jesus called His disciples to Him and said, "This woman has given more than anyone. The others gave out of their wealth, but this woman gave all that she had."

You see, Jesus is more interested in the giver's *heart* than in the *amount* of the gift.

Last year, when my church was raising money to build an addition to the sanctuary, I saved up $26.75. That's a mite compared to what some people gave, and I'm sure it only paid for about three bricks, but I worked really hard for that money. I had two bake sales and mowed three yards. (Who knew burned brownies wouldn't be a runaway hit?)

Like Mr. Kinnear explained, I gave what I could, and that is what matters to Jesus. That makes a mite downright mighty.

A Meal Not to Be Missed

Matthew 26; Mark 14; Luke 22; John 13

T he last days Jesus walked on the earth were really, really important. And I bet they were super hard for Jesus. If that had been me, knowing what was coming, I would have felt like I had a bowling ball in my stomach the whole time.

> **WOW. THIS DEFINITELY WAS NOT THE NIGHT TO BE LATE FOR DINNER!**

Jesus knew He was leaving earth to go home to heaven, but He wanted His twelve disciples to learn some very important things first—things they would need after He was gone. He told them they would not eat and drink together like this again until they met in His Father's kingdom.

During this special dinner, Jesus surprised the disciples by standing up from the table, getting a bowl of water, and carefully washing their feet.

It might have creeped me out a little if someone started scrubbing my dirty feet, but servants typically washed people's feet to remove the grime of the day. So this whole thing really bugged the disciples. Jesus was their master, a king, and *He* was washing their feet?!

No! Let me wash Your feet.

Jesus told His disciples not to worry and to let Him wash their feet—then to follow His example once He was gone.

When the feast was over and there was nothing left but bread and wine, Jesus did another really, really important thing: He took the bread and broke it into pieces and gave a piece to each disciple, saying, "This is My body." They ate the bread together. He then poured wine and said, "Drink from it, all of you. This is my blood of the covenant, which is poured out for many for the forgiveness of sins." And they all drank.

Then things got really awkward. During dinner, Jesus told the disciples that one of them would betray Him. Can you imagine the looks that must have shot around the room? They all denied they would ever betray Jesus. But Jesus singled out Judas, and Judas bolted from the table and ran out into the night.

Every time communion happens at church, I think about what it would have been like to be at that first communion WITH JESUS.

Draw Here↓

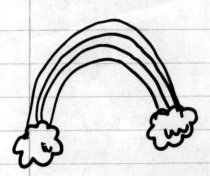

The Only Way

John 14-16

It was a lot to handle. First, there was the Last Supper, the feet washing, and Jesus talking about leaving the disciples. Then Jesus continued to talk to His disciples about them denying that they ever knew Him.

They just couldn't get it—kind of like me and earth science. The disciples were trying their hardest, but they couldn't understand everything Jesus was saying. But they would understand more over the next few days.

During the Last Supper, Jesus gave His disciples a road map they could follow in case they ever felt lost. He knew their panic was setting in.

"Don't let your hearts be troubled. Trust in God. And trust in me. There are many rooms in my Father's house. I would not tell you this if it were not true. I am going there to prepare a place for you. After I go and prepare a place for you, I will come back. Then I will take you to be with me so that you may be where I am."

But Thomas basically told Jesus, "No, we don't really know the way, Jesus! We need you to tell us!"

"I am the way. And I am the truth and the life," Jesus said. "The only way to the Father is through me."

Philip asked Jesus to show them the Father, but Jesus answered, "I've been with you all this time, and you still don't know Me? Anyone who has seen Me has seen the Father."

That was it! The truth clicked like peanut butter and chocolate. After all that time, they finally got it and said, "Now we understand. You really did come from God."

Jesus also promised the disciples that the Holy Spirit would be with them, to guide and help them figure things out after He was gone.

What an awesome gift—and one the disciples could never, ever in a million years forget!

Jesus was getting ready to go to the cross and die for our sins, and He spent his last hours giving to His followers. Guiding them. Comforting them. That is really big love.

Jesus is the real thing!

ZZZZZZ o o o

Matthew 26; Mark 14; Luke 22

The story about Jesus praying in the Garden of Gethsemane before He was taken prisoner makes me mad. There, I said it. In fact, the story makes me want to put the disciples in a giant catapult and send them to the moon. Judas wasn't the only disciple who broke the Bro Code that night. All of the disciples let Jesus down.

I get that they had just had a big meal and were tired, but did they really have to fall asleep when Jesus needed them the most? Yeah. That's what happened. *The disciples were catching ZZZZs.*

After the Last Supper, Jesus went with the disciples to the Garden called Gethsemane and said, "Sit here while I go pray." His heart was very troubled. In fact, He said, "I am full of sorrow. My heart is breaking with sadness. Stay here and watch."

Jesus knew the danger ahead. The Pharisees wanted Him dead. He would soon be crucified.

He cried out to God with all His heart that night. He also let God know that He understood and accepted His mission—even if it was going to be terrible, awful, and beyond cruel. He knew that His life would be an exchange for all of humankind's sin and would make things right between God and humans again. The pain was worth it to Him.

Jesus stopped praying and went to find His disciples, who were, like I said, sleeping. This happened not once, but three times!

I get so steamed when I read this story. Not cool, disciples. Not cool.

But then I think to myself, *Ned, how many times have you not done the simplest things God has asked you to do?*

C'mon, dudes. Snap out of it!

Judas Sells Out

Matthew 26; Mark 14; Luke 22; John 18

L ast year, at our family reunion, there was lots of food, lots of laughter, and lots of relatives telling me how "handsome" I had become. I'm not gonna lie. It was a good day to be Ned Wiley.

I was one of the oldest of the cousins there, so I took it upon myself to show the younger Wileys how to live large. Eating Jell-O is boring . . . unless you do it with your hands tied behind your back. So I got about six of us together and we climbed into my tree house, where we went crazy slurping, gulping, and inhaling my Aunt Sue's ginormous tangerine Jell-O salad.

I thought I was the slurp king, but my second cousin Dewey made me look as reserved as the Prince of Wales. That kid was born to slurp, burp, and gulp in large quantities.

About two hours (and a few green-around-the-gills cousins) later, Aunt Sue came looking for her Jell-O salad. No one said a word. She scanned our faces like she was studying a police lineup. Then she offered anyone with information about the disappearance of her Jell-O salad a reward: an ice-cold rocket pop! That was it. I knew I was a goner.

Not ratting out your friends is like "Friendship 101." It's break-ing Bro Code for sure. ⬅

Dewey squeaked, jumped, and flipped like a Chihuahua. "It was Ned! It was Ned! He forced us to eat your Jell-O! And I threw up! It was Ned!" (Did he mention it was Ned?)

I was sold down the river for a rocket pop. Go figure.

Let me just say: that family reunion escapade was nowhere NEAR the betrayal of Jesus.

I can't imagine how Jesus must have felt when He was given up by one of His best friends. I'm sure it must have broken His heart when His dear friend, His own disciple Judas, betrayed him to the Roman soldiers.

Judas had gone to the chief priests and asked, "What will you give me if I turn Jesus over to you?" They promised him thirty pieces of silver. Can you imagine selling out your best friend for a few pieces of silver? Or handing over *Jesus* for any amount of money?

After leaving the Upper Room, where they had shared their last meal, Jesus took His disciples to the Garden of Gethsemane to pray.

Jesus could hear His betrayer coming and could see torches blazing into the night. Judas stepped toward Jesus and kissed him on the cheek—a signal to the soldiers that He was Jesus.

Jesus said, "Judas, do you betray the Son of man with a kiss?"

The soldiers grabbed Jesus and took Him away.

No Way: Peter Denies Jesus

Matthew 26; Mark 14; Luke 22; John 18

Have you ever been embarrassed by someone and pretended not to know them? Penelope did that to me when we went to the mall with Mom when I was about seven years old. You see, I used to love wearing my Superman costume all the time, and I would run around with my arms out, pretending to fly and trying to rescue people. When I tried to "save" a little old lady and accidentally knocked her and her walker into the mall fountain instead, Penelope walked right out of the mall and waited in the car for over an hour so no one would know she was with me. Mom couldn't even coax her out with the promise of new jeans—that was some serious embarrassment.

Peter and Penelope have that denial thing in common. The big difference is that I was a silly kid pretending to be a superhero and Jesus is the greatest superhero ever. Jesus had actually predicted that Peter would deny Him three times before a rooster crowed. But Peter refused to believe Him. "No way!" Peter insisted. "I'd even die with You." Of course, Jesus knew what He was talking about, and right after He was arrested, the denials started.

Peter was waiting near the place where Jesus was being questioned, and a servant girl asked, "Weren't you with Jesus?"

"I don't know Him," said Peter (*ding-ding-ding* #1!). Later, someone else asked the same thing, and once again Peter denied knowing Jesus (*ding-ding-ding* #2!).

An hour later, another person spoke to Peter. "Surely you're one of Jesus' followers. You even talk like them."

"I don't know what you're talking about!" cried Peter (*ding-ding-ding* #3!).

Just then a rooster crowed, and Peter remembered Jesus' words. Realizing what he had done, Peter went off by himself and cried bitterly.

I know it's tempting to really sock it to Peter here and call him a wishy-washy disciple. But here's the truth: Peter only denied Jesus *three* times; most of us have denied him *three hundred times*. Think about it . . .

I remember on the bus one day Howie Doohan looked me straight in the eye and asked me in a kind of a whisper, "Okay, squirt, what's the deal with this Jesus guy?" This was the one day out of 365 that he *wasn't* being mean. I could tell he really and truly wanted to know.

I had a million things to say to Howie and all of them rushed up to my throat like a stampede of bulls. Honest, they did. But the only thing that came out was a nervous squeak that sounded something like, "Eh."

"Eh? What's that sup-posed to mean? Eh? What a dweeb!" said Howie, laugh-ing hysterically and raising his voice.

I felt like I'd let Jesus down. But next time I'll be ready. I've been practicing what to say, and I've made it my mission to tell Howie all about how awesome Jesus is. Luckily, Peter got lots of second chances to tell people about Jesus, and so will I!

Justice Was Not Served

Matthew 27; Mark 15; Luke 23; John 19

I know I've made some jokes and drawn some funny pictures about Bible stories, but there isn't anything funny about these next few stories. They just make me really sad, even though I know that they are the most important stories in the Bible (and probably in the entire history of the world). Keep reading, but don't say I didn't warn you about how difficult they are.

After Judas told the soldiers where to find Jesus, they led Jesus to the religious leaders, who decided that Jesus needed to die because He was claiming to be the Son of God, and they did not believe Him. The next day they took Him to the palace of Pontius Pilate. Pilate was the head honcho with the power to say who was guilty and who wasn't—kinda like a judge and jury all rolled into one. Pilate realized quickly that many of the leaders in the area really hated Jesus. They told Pilate that Jesus, who claimed to be "the king of the Jews," was a threat to Roman rule, hoping this would get Pilate really mad.

Pilate asked Jesus tons of questions, but Jesus didn't try to defend Himself. When asked if He was King of the Jews, Jesus said yes. He was a king, but His kingdom was not of this world, He explained. Pilate couldn't find any real charges against Jesus. Still the crowd was yelling, demanding that Jesus be punished. Pilate asked the crowd, "What do you want me to do with Him?"

Pilate knew that the religious leaders didn't have the authority to kill Jesus; they were under Roman law and needed the Roman governor to give the order. He understood that the whole "trial" was a sham, a fake, but the crowd was loud and mean and Pilate was nervous that they would turn on him.

The crowd kept yelling. When given the choice by Pilate to release Jesus or Barabbas, a known murderer, the crowd shocked Pilate: "Release Barabbas and crucify Jesus."

Pilate asked, "Why? What has He done?"

But they just yelled louder, "Crucify Him!"

Pilate gave in to the crowd. He tried just having Jesus whipped publicly and handed Him over to the soldiers. The soldiers also made fun of Jesus, mocking Him and calling Him names. They put a purple robe on Him and shoved a crown made out of sharp thorns on His head. They hit Him in the face, spit on Him, and yelled, "Hail, king of the Jews!"

But none of that was enough for the angry religious leaders, and the peer pressure finally got to Pilate. He handed Jesus over to the priests to be crucified.

The Worst Day Ever

Matthew 27; Mark 15; Luke 23; John 19

This is the most difficult part of the Bible for me to read. It's super painful and upsetting to truly picture Jesus, who came to teach us love and mercy, getting bullied, beaten up, and killed in a really awful, terrible way. It's like all the bullies in the universe had a convention in Jerusalem, and Jesus walked into the middle of it. It's just NOT FAIR!

But fair or not, the crucifixion story is important to read. Every. Word. Of. It.

Crucifixion was the way Romans killed criminals. After His "trial," Jesus was forced (like any other murderer or thief) to carry a heavy wooden cross up the hill while everyone watched.

Jesus was then laid on the cross, where his feet and hands were nailed to it. The cross was raised and put in the ground. It was a slow, agonizing, brutal way to die.

Jesus was crucified that day with two other people—both criminals, one on each side of Him. One of the thieves next to Jesus made fun of Him. The other said, "We deserve to die, but this man has done no wrong." He then asked Jesus to remember him in His kingdom. Jesus told him, "Today you'll be with Me in paradise."

Pilate wrote a sign that said "KING OF THE JEWS" to place on top of Jesus' cross. This made the religious leaders mad, but Pilate ignored them.

The soldiers took Jesus clothes and cast "lots" for them, which is basically like playing rock-paper-scissors to see who would get what. He wasn't even dead yet and they were already fighting over his possessions.

Despite being tortured, mocked, and wrongly accused, as Jesus hung on the cross, He prayed, "Forgive them, Father. They don't know what they're doing."

Then Jesus cried out to heaven, "It is finished," and He gave up His spirit.

The sky grew dark, the earth shook, and the curtain of the Jewish temple was torn from top to bottom. One Roman standing near the cross said to his soldiers, "This man truly was the Son of God."

It was the worst, saddest day ever, but in some ways it was also the best day ever. Jesus came to earth to be punished and die for our sins so that we could all be forgiven, and it was all part of God's plan—even the really bad parts. God sacrificed His only Son so we could be with Him, which makes that day pretty amazing after all.

Jesus Is Buried in a Tomb

Matthew 27; Mark 15; Luke 23; John 19

Joseph of Arimathea was a rich man who had followed Jesus in secret because he feared the religious officials. After the crucifixion, Joseph asked Pilate if he could care for Jesus' body, and Pilate let him. Joseph was *really* brave to go to Pilate and ask to do this. Most of Jesus' disciples had already fled for fear of being associated with Jesus. They knew they might be killed if anyone found them. For Joseph to step up took major courage . . . and love.

Joseph made sure that Jesus' body was cleaned, wrapped in a fresh white cloth, and rubbed with herbs and sweet-smelling oils. A man named Nicodemus also came and helped prepare the body for burial. The men then laid Jesus' body in a special tomb Joseph had bought for himself that was carved from solid rock.

Then a large stone was placed in front of the opening to the tomb. The Pharisees (religious leaders) asked Pilate to place guards at the tomb to make sure that no one could steal Jesus' body and then claim that he had risen.

What they didn't understand is that there's not a rock, guard, or grave on earth that can hold Jesus Christ! The best day was about to happen . . .

The Best Day Ever

Matthew 28; Mark 16; Luke 24; John 20

kay, I'm pretty big on happy endings—scratch that, *hopeful* endings—especially after all that Jesus went through to sacrifice Himself for us! I'm happy to report news that I'm sure (or I hope) you've already heard:

On the third day, after His crucifixion and burial, Jesus rose from the dead!

And I don't mean like a made-believe zombie or a vampire in a horror movie—I mean, Jesus was alive and completely Himself. It was the greatest miracle EVER!

Here's what happened: after the Sabbath, several of the women who had followed Jesus went to the tomb early in the morning. They bought spices so they could anoint Jesus' body, but when they reached the tomb, the stone had been rolled away. As they entered the tomb, they saw an angel in a white robe and were frightened.

"Don't be alarmed," the angel said. "You are looking for Jesus who was crucified. He is risen! He is not here." He then told them to go tell the disciples that they would see Jesus again in Galilee just as He promised.

The resurrection is SO huge—God is bigger than death, bigger than our sin. The resurrection shows us that Jesus kept His word to rise from the dead. That He has gone on to rule heaven. That we will be resurrected with Him someday (if we believe Him and follow Him). And that God's power is available to us as His followers!

How totally awesome is that? Jesus' resurrection, which we celebrate each year on Easter Sunday, is definitely the *best day ever*!

Welcome Back, Jesus

Matthew 28; Mark 16; Luke 24; John 20

So the tomb was empty, and Jesus had come back to earth like He said He would. And then He met with His disciples. If I had been there, here's my Top Three List of what I might have said to Jesus:

> **3. Welcome back, Lord! I'd love to see Your slide show of heaven. I'll bring the popcorn!**
>
> **2. I knew You would return! I've been working on an awesome "Welcome Back" sign.**

And the number one thing I'd say—in all seriousness:

> **1. Thank You, Jesus. You're the best. Like, thank You times A MILLION! Thank You, thank You, thank You!**

I'm sure "I'm sorry" was a MAJOR part of what the disciples were thinking when Jesus appeared to them the first time. The first thing Jesus said to them was: "Peace be with you."

Don't forget, most of these guys had scrammed like scared rabbits when Jesus was being crucified, and they still weren't 100 percent in agreement about what had happened. They were grieving that Jesus was dead, and they were confused. They missed Him. But His first words to them after an intense three-day weekend were really amazing: *peace be unto you.*

Still, seeing Jesus in the flesh scared the disciples. It would probably scare me too!

"Why are you so troubled?" Jesus asked. "Look at My hands and

My feet, and you will see that it is Me. Touch Me, and you'll know that I am not a spirit. A spirit doesn't have flesh and bones."

Those confused guys took it all in . . .

And then it clicked. It really was the Lord. The disciples were overjoyed. Jesus had returned from the dead, just as He had promised, and He was right there with them.

Then, like any wiped-out pal would, Jesus asked, "Hey, do you have anything to eat?"

They gave Him broiled fish, and He began to talk with His friends about the Scriptures . . .

Doubting Thomas Doubts No More

John 20

I used to wonder where the expression "doubting Thomas" came from. You know, when someone won't believe something until he sees it for himself. Kinda like when I told Austin about the two-foot-long snake I found down at the creek. Seriously, the thing was huge. It was awesome/gross. But ol' Ain't-Believing-You Austin thought I was making it up! Until I popped open the lid on that shoe box and about scared the pants off him! You'd better believe Austin isn't a skeptic now!

> YOU CAN BET NO ONE WAS CALLING AUSTIN "BLESSED" AFTER HE RAN SCREAMING LIKE A GIRL WHEN HE SAW THAT SCALY WONDER OF NATURE.

One of the disciples, Thomas, was not in the room when Jesus returned the first time. So when the rest of the disciples reported back to Thomas that they had seen the Lord, he wasn't convinced. "Until I put my finger in the mark of the nails in His hands and place my hand on His side (where the sword went in), I will not believe." He needed a faith infusion.

Eight days passed. Again, the disciples were together in a room. The door was shut and Jesus appeared out of nowhere. This time Thomas was there. Jesus said to Thomas, "Go ahead. Put your finger on My hands and your hand on My side. Do not doubt but believe."

You know how this story ends. Yeah, Thomas became one of the BIGGEST believers ever!

Then Jesus said something really cool to Thomas, and it applies to people like you and me—and everyone, actually. "Because you have seen Me," Jesus said, "it's easy for you to believe in Me. Blessed are those who believe even though they don't see Me."

If I read that right, it says *I'm* blessed because I didn't have to put my finger in the nail holes in Jesus' hands to believe in Him and His resurrection. Believing in Jesus without "proof" takes a lot of faith. That's the kind of Jesus follower I want to be!

Gospel World Tour

Matthew 28; Mark 16; Luke 24; Acts 1

Jesus talked with His disciples for forty days after He rose from the dead. Mostly He talked about the kingdom of God.

Once Jesus made it clear that the kingdom of heaven wasn't on earth, He shared probably the biggest and most important message ever as He taught the disciples in those last visits they had together: we're supposed to tell people about Jesus and about heaven. We're actually supposed to tell *the whole world*.

Kinda like if I tried to convince Superman that he really wasn't from Planet Krypton but was actually from Tampa. That conversation would be short . . . and end with a big thud!

I look at it as my biggest ops mission ever—to go on a Jesus World Tour and to share His love wherever I can.

Makes sense to me. Jesus suffered a horrible death to give people the chance to know God, to be forgiven for their sins, and to spend *forever* in heaven with Him. Getting the word out is a HUGE deal!

It's called the Great Commission. Jesus basically told the disciples that their main job was to share their experiences with Jesus and what He did in their lives so that others could know Him too.

I think people overcomplicate that sometimes. I sure overcomplicated it on the bus that day with Howie Doohan. I choked like I had just inhaled a Corn Nut when he asked me who Jesus was. But once I recovered, I realized that God can help me with this. You won't always tell people about Jesus with the perfect words. But God will be there with you, and He will fill in the gaps. And it will get easier every time you share.

When you think about it, it's the coolest mission we could be given: just share. And I've always wanted to buy one of those around-the-world plane tickets. Ned Wiley: Jesus World Tour. Coming to a city near you!

Draw Here!

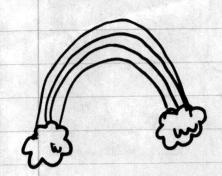

201

Jesus Goes to Heaven

Mark 16; Luke 24; Acts 1

At church one Sunday I heard the word *ascension*. You know where this is going. Yeah, smarty pants. I had to look it up. Basically it means this: to go up from earth to heaven. **← ALSO, only one guy has ever done it: Jesus.**

But let's backtrack for a second. Before Jesus went up to heaven, He told the disciples that while John the Baptist used water to baptize, they would be baptized in the Holy Spirit and receive the power they needed to do the things He was asking them to do. How cool is that? With the Holy Spirit they could go, do, achieve! The mission—the *Great Commission*—looked totally different with a holy partner to help.

I dream all the time about what kind of superpower I, Ned Wiley, would like to have if I were given the chance to fight the forces of darkness on earth. But when I think about all of the coolest ones—flying, being invisible, being made of steel—none of those is nearly as cool as the ultimate superpower designed by God: walking with the Holy Spirit. The Holy Spirit is real, and He comes to live inside you.

THE HOLY SPIRIT CAN HELP ANYONE—EVEN A SCRAWNY TWELVE-YEAR-OLD WITH GLASSES.

Jesus said that the disciples would be bold witnesses to the farthest parts of the world, but they weren't to go until they were officially "given" the Holy Spirit. With those final words, Jesus went up to heaven—ascended right before their very eyes. Can you imagine how awesome that must have been?

And then the disciples waited . . . for the amazing thing Jesus had promised.

Holy Spirit Onboard

Acts 1-2

After Jesus appeared to the disciples and then ascended to heaven, the disciples went back to Jerusalem. This was risky because Jesus had been crucified there, and lots of people still hated Him and His followers. Would they be arrested? They went anyway. Jesus had risen from the dead, had come to them in the flesh, and had told them what to do. They were changed—forever. What could any bully do to them now?

Once they were back in Jerusalem, Jesus' followers met in an upstairs room to wait and pray for the Holy Spirit to come.

And boy, did the Spirit come! It's kind hard to explain, but disciples heard the sound of a "mighty rushing wind" and saw little tongues of fire over the head of each person. Crazy, right? But when you hang with Jesus, you'd better be prepared for anything!

Austin and I thought we'd try to figure out this "tongues of fire" business. A jalapeño pepper and two crying kids later, we realized we might have misunderstood.

What do you think you'd do if you had been there? The disciples started praising God! Then they went to the streets below, where a bunch of people had gathered. The disciples spoke in different languages, but somehow everyone understood their words.

Peter stepped up to preach and everyone listened. They began to truly understand Peter's words. He told them that by crucifying Jesus, they had killed the Son of God. And the people began to repent and were baptized. About *three thousand* came to know the TRUTH about Jesus that day!

That's what the Holy Spirit does. He opens eyes, ears, and hearts that were once totally glued shut. Pretty amazing, huh?

The Holy Spirit also bonds people together. It doesn't matter how different they are—they can be kind to each other.

When the Holy Spirit came that day, Jesus' followers bonded together in a whole new way and started forming communities where they would share food and care for one another. And that was the beginning of the church.

The Holy Spirit could bond even me and Howie Doohan. I just know it.

Stephen: Bully Magnet

Acts 6-8

You would think that the word of Jesus' resurrection and the Holy Spirit coming down into Jerusalem would make things easier for Christians, but instead, things just got harder. We've had a bunch of assemblies at school about bullying, and let me tell you, the Christians back then were definitely being bullied. And I'm not just talking steal-your-lunch-money-and-give-you-a-wedgie bullying either—this was serious stuff.

One of the first bullying victims was Stephen. He was a really dedicated Christian (Dad calls him an *evangelist*, which apparently means he talked **← It's bad when having your underwear pulled up to your ears actually sounds like your idea of a good time.** about Jesus to everyone he met) and worked around the clock to spread the word about Jesus to others.

When Stephen went to the synagogue to preach, the Jewish leaders got really angry. See, God had given Stephen a special gift to preach, and the leaders knew people were listening. Remember: many of the Jewish leaders did NOT believe that Jesus was the Son of God, so they told everyone that Stephen was a liar.

The leaders hired men in the crowd to go wherever Stephen went and accuse him of lying. The men spread rumors about Stephen. "We have heard Stephen speak against God and Moses."

This made the crowd angry, and Stephen was brought before a council. When the high priest accused Stephen, he just repeated familiar scriptures and reminded people what happens when you disobey God. He wasn't afraid. Like, not afraid at all! Of course, this just made the council angrier—bullies really get mad when you aren't afraid of them.

206

God totally had Stephen's back. God even gave him a VIP peek at heaven while he stood before the bullies. As Stephen talked of heaven and what he saw, the furious men picked up stones and threw them at him until Stephen died.

Stephen was the first man killed for preaching about Jesus.

At that stoning was a Jewish Pharisee named Saul. Saul was one of the biggest bullies around. He was determined to destroy the church and went from house to house sending anyone who followed Jesus to prison. Saul was a strict Jew and a leading Jewish ruler. He was crazy zealous about following the law of Moses. But as you'll see, Saul is proof that even the most hardened heart can go from a swirly-giving-trash-talking-meanie to all-around amazing person when God gets involved. Read on to find out more . . .

Saul Sees the Light

Acts 9

O kay, so we've already established that so far Saul has been pretty successful at terrorizing and locking up every Christian he could find. But that all changed one day when Saul was on his way to Damascus. To do what? Round up, hassle, and imprison Christians—what else!

I'm telling you, this guy could have taught professional bullying classes. You know, like "Swirlies 101" and "Wet Willies 203."

While Saul made his way along the road, a fantastical, mind-blowing, out-of-this-world, only-God-can-do-this thing happened! A bright light came from heaven and a voice spoke to Saul: "Saul, Saul, why are you persecuting Me?"

Oh man, oh man, oh man! I wish I had been there! It's like God rolled up a giant newspaper and smacked Saul upside the head. I bet Saul thought he was going bonkers!

Saul was shocked and terrified and fell on the ground. "Who are you?" he cried out. (Of course, it was God. Who else could break open the sky and call your name?)

"I am Jesus. I am the One you are trying to hurt," the voice answered."

When Saul got to his feet, he realized that he couldn't see. The Lord told him to go into the city, so men led him into Damascus.

A man named Ananias took Paul in and took care of him. For the next three days, Saul was completely blind while God worked on transforming him from a zero to a hero. Ananias laid his hands on Saul and told him that Jesus had given him the power to help him see again and be filled with the Holy Spirit.

Instantly, Saul realized what a horrible guy he'd been, and he was super embarrassed and regretful. In that moment, he knew he had been wrong. Really, really wrong. Saul did an instant 180-degree turnaround.

It would be like Darth Vader suddenly turning from the dark side or the Joker suddenly teaming up with Batman. Totally super cool, right?

Later, Saul was called Paul and became one of the greatest ever missionaries of the Christian faith. Seriously, he was an all-out superhero.

Paul went everywhere—and got bullied a lot himself—to get out the word about Jesus. Some people didn't trust him at first because of his instant turnaround. But after a while, while Paul became a loved and respected Christian leader.

I wonder if it's wrong for me to pray that crazy Howie Doohan has his own Damascus Road moment soon? He lives on Milky Way Road, so I guess that would make it a Milky Way moment, although that sounds like an awesome moment involving a delicious candy bar.

Even if that *doesn't* happen and he keeps bullying me, I know I'll survive. I can handle being called a "Jesus freak" and getting the occasional wedgie. I'm not going to let that stop me from telling other kids about Jesus.

And I'll trust God to talk to Howie Doohan.

Draw Here↓

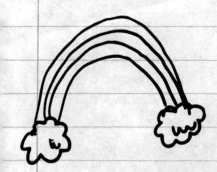

Jailbird Missionaries

Acts 16

Paul traveled all over, spreading the news about Jesus, and his travels took him to some pretty cool places. At one point, Paul traveled to Macedonia with another missionary named Silas.

There they went to the city of Philippi. A slave girl who was filled with an evil spirit shouted nasty things at Paul and Silas every time they passed her. The evil spirit made her mean. Paul got fed up with the taunting pretty fast and commanded the spirit to come out of the girl. And it did!

But when the spirit left, the slave girl's owners got really angry. The owners weren't shy about telling everyone how mad they were, and that caused a lot of trouble for Paul and Silas.

A super angry mob dragged Paul and Silas through the streets and took them to city leaders, who had them beaten and threw them in prison.

← **Yeah, lots of angry mobs in the New Testament, huh?**

I don't know about you, but the only mob I've ever seen was a flash mob that some of the adults at church did during Vacation Bible School. They all just started singing and dancing to old hymns at snack time. Have you ever seen your mom do the robot in a room full of people? It was seriously embarrassing.

I whined a lot about that flash mob and tried to forbid my mom from ever dancing in public again, but Paul and Silas didn't complain at all about the mob throwing them in jail. They spent their days worshipping God and singing about His goodness. The people of Philippi didn't know what to do with them.

One night, as Paul and Silas sang praises, the earth shook and the doors of the prison flew open! The chains on their feet even fell to the ground! They were free—but none of the prisoners even moved from their cells.

The jailer knew he was in deep trouble when he arrived and saw the prison doors wide open. He figured all the prisoners had escaped and knew he would be put to death as punishment for letting them get away, so he decided to kill himself. Just then, Paul spoke up and told him, "Don't harm yourself. We are all here."

And it was true—all the prisoners were accounted for. The jailer knew then that they really were men of God. Paul and Silas told them, "Believe in the Lord Jesus and you will be saved."

Paul and Silas baptized the jailer and his whole family before daybreak! The jailer took Paul and Silas to his house, bandaged their wounds, and treated them as guests.

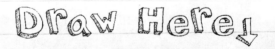

Draw Here!

Paul Gets Shipwrecked

Acts 27-28

Paul faced a lot of hard times as a Christian. He was constantly put in jail for preaching. Not to mention all the times he got beat up for being a vocal Jesus follower or all the nights he didn't have food to eat or a safe place to sleep. But Paul wasn't like other people. He didn't quit when things got hard. He loved God and knew he was on a mission for Him. He was dedicated to completing that mission, no matter how difficult and uncomfortable it was.

At one point, Paul was arrested and put on a ship bound for Rome with some other prisoners. He was under the guard of a centurion named Julius. Along the journey, Paul warned Julius that the ship should not sail a certain route because it was too dangerous, but Julius ignored him.

A horrible storm came up! The men threw everything they could overboard to lighten the ship, but nothing helped. They were sure the ship would be crushed by the waves and they would all drown.

← Paul had warned those knuckleheads.

Now, this seems seriously terrifying to me. Giant waves washing over the deck and *crushing* the boat? The one time at summer camp when my canoe capsized, I screamed and splashed and flailed and thought I was a goner for sure—until I remembered the water only came up to my waist.

Luckily, Paul was a lot braver than I am! He told the people on the ship, "I said not to come this way, but you didn't listen. But don't worry. Be of good cheer. God has shown me that the ship will be wrecked, but everyone onboard will be spared and make it safely to an island."

And it happened just as Paul said. The ship wrecked, but all 276 people made it safely to the island of Malta.

God used Paul's shipwreck to bring the gospel to the island of Malta.

Draw Here↓

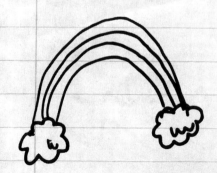

217

Paul Survives a Snakebite

Acts 28

When Paul made it to shore of Malta, the islanders were very nice to him and the other castaways.

The castaways were all cold and wet, so the islanders built a fire and welcomed them. Paul was carrying a bundle of sticks, and as he put it on the fire, the heat caused a poisonous snake called a viper to jump out, wrap around his hand, and bite him!

The islanders were very superstitious. They saw Paul's snakebite as a sign that Paul must be a murderer and thought that, even though he survived the shipwreck, "justice" had caught up to him. Instead, Paul surprised them all and flung the poisonous snake off his hand. The people expected Paul to swell up like a blowfish or plop over dead.

A giant snake jumps up and bites me? That's where I lose my mind. But not Paul.

But what they didn't know was that God had promised Paul safe passage from that raging sea, and that's exactly what God was going to give him. Paul was just fine—he didn't even get sick!

When God is up to big things, you can bet that the small things—like a deadly snake (or any other annoying person or situation)—isn't going to get in His way. He's got your back.

The World Before Text Messages

Paul's life was kind of amazing. He started out persecuting Jesus' followers, but once he gave his life to God, he went wherever God called him to go. He traveled all over the place, stood before kings, survived shipwrecks—he had one crazy adventure after another. Sometimes things got pretty rough—check out 2 Corinthians 11:16–33 to see just how hard Paul's journey was. But he also said that he considered it a joy to suffer for Christ and was grateful to God always.

One of the greatest things about Paul's life is that what he did nearly two thousand years ago is still helping people today. How cool is that, right? I would love to do something that would still be helping people in two thousand years. You see, God spoke to Paul and wanted him to send His messages to early Christians in letters, which he wrote on scrolls.

These letters later became some of the books of the New Testament. It was really, really important that Paul write these letters.

Planes, cars, cell phones, and the Internet didn't exist back then. Paul couldn't e-mail or text people, and even if he could go visit them, it took a loooooong time to get there. Plus, if he had just told people, the messages could have gotten really messed up. Have you ever played the telephone game, where one person whispers a phrase to another person? You say something like, "I love to play

silly games with hair gel," and then that person whispers it to the next person and so on. By the time the message gets to the last person, they think the message was, "I love to eat moldy cheese at Taco Bell." Confusing, huh?

So Paul wrote down letters to encourage the churches he had started. He urged them to keep the faith and be united in their love for one another and for God. He gave them messages God gave him so they could follow God's plan and not be led astray.

Paul's letters had *a lot* of important stuff from God. Here are a few of the highlights:

- All people are sinners.
- Everyone deserves to be punished for his or her sins.
- God gave us His only Son, Jesus, to die in place of our eternal punishment.
- If you believe in Jesus and ask God to forgive your sins, He will forgive you.
- God will then give you the Holy Spirit to live in your heart.
- The Holy Spirit will help you out. Every day. Big time. Until you go to heaven. And live with Jesus. Forever.

How simple is that?

I'm just glad they *didn't* have cell phones back then. If Paul had texted his message the Bible might say:

All peeps r sinners.

Every1 deserves 2 b punished 4 sins

God gave us His Son, Jesus, 2 die n place of our punishment

If u believe n Jesus and ask God 2 forgive ur sins, u won't b punished

You get the idea . . .

But I've gotta say, I prefer Paul's version.

Draw Here!

Don't Call It a Comeback

The Book of Revelation

I've got big news for you guys: Jesus is coming back. That's right. It's all written out in the book of Revelation—the very last book in the Bible. Of course, it isn't really a comeback since Jesus is always with us in our hearts.

Jesus' disciple John wrote the book of Revelation when he was a prisoner on the island of Patmos. He was sent there because he believed in Jesus and, like the other disciples, refused to zip his lip about Him (surprise, surprise!).

John had a lot of time to think while he was on this island. In that time, he was given a message by God, a vision of what's to come. The book of Revelation is the record of everything God told John that day. By the way, I had to **Kind of like** look up *revelation*, and here's **a treasure** what it means: "explaining **map. How** what once was secret." So the *whole book* is showing **cool is that?** us something that used to be secret.

John wasn't exactly sipping fruity drinks and snorkeling.

Revelation says that when Jesus returns, believers will rejoice, but God's enemies will be shaking in their boots. I'm not gonna lie. Some of the stuff in Revelation is kinda scary, but a lot of it is really awesome too. Here's a little of what John saw:

He saw the door of heaven open up and a voice call him. He saw people dressed in white and wearing crowns. Other heavenly beings were there, and everyone was worshipping God. He saw heavenly beings bow down and worship Jesus, and he saw a city of God more beautiful than anything he'd ever laid eyes on. John saw believers enter into heaven and crystal water flowing through the city.

What did John do when he saw all of this? I guess what we'd all do. He fell down and worshipped too! Jesus told him that the invitation to heaven is for all people (not just the cool kids). But only those

who hear and obey can share in its blessings. Then Jesus made this cool and amazing promise: "Surely, I come quickly."

I like what Mr. Kinnear, my youth leader, said when I asked him about the book of Revelation: "It's about Jesus coming back to fix up this really broken place. It's Jesus saying to us all, 'I'm on My way. Don't worry. I'll be there sooner than you think.'"

I really like that. And I'm waiting.

Did you hear that, Jesus? Ned Wiley is waiting for You (that's 2613 McDoogal Court). And I can't wait to meet You in person. I know it's going to be the best day ever, whether it's tomorrow or in ninety years.

Draw Here

Draw Here↓

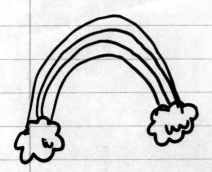